AMERICA...

"hanging by a thread."

RICHARD MCKENZIE NEAL

authorHOUSE®

AuthorHouse™
1663 Liberty Drive
Bloomington, IN 47403
www.authorhouse.com
Phone: 1-800-839-8640

Published by AuthorHouse 7/9/2012

ISBN: 978-1-4772-2936-1 (sc)
ISBN: 978-1-4772-2935-4 (hc)
ISBN: 978-1-4772-2934-7 (e)

Library of Congress Control Number: 2012911612

Preamble

'You see...if everyone is special, then no one is really special. If everyone gets a trophy, trophies become meaningless.

In an unspoken but not so subtle Darwinian competition with one another...which I think springs from the fear of our own insignificance, exists a subset of dread... of our personal mortality that we have acknowledged of late. We Americans, to our detriment, have come to value accolades more than genuine achievement.'

FOREWORD

To paraphrase the now extinct dinosaur, "OMG! Didn't see that coming! How could this have happened... aren't we too big to fail?"

Of course younger generations would correctly point out that every passing generation predicts our world is going to Hell in a hand basket. In the 50s many Americans were thoroughly convinced that Elvis was the antichrist and that he was there with his rock and roll music and suggestive onstage dance gyrations to lead their young people into eternal damnation. And I'm still not sure they weren't right...

There have been many contributing factors to our descent into this black hole: A region of space-time from which nothing, not even light, can escape.

I can accept that Franklin Roosevelt is consistently rated by scholars as one of the top three United States Presidents, but history continues to reveal how the best of intentions have a way of morphing into aberrations with little resemblance to the original feel good objectives.

1935: President Franklin Roosevelt, in his State of the

Union address, called for legislation to provide assistance for the jobless, elderly, impoverished, children and the handicapped.

1941: President Franklin Roosevelt, in his State of the Union address, outlined a goal of Four Freedoms: freedom of speech and expression, freedom of people to worship God in their own way, "freedom from want" and "freedom from fear."

1960s: The Great Society was a set of domestic programs in the United States promoted by President Lyndon B. Johnson and fellow Democrats in Congress. The two main goals of the Great Society social reforms were the elimination of poverty and racial injustice. New major spending programs that addressed education, medical care, urban problems, and transportation were launched during this period. The Great Society, in scope and sweep, resembled the New Deal domestic agenda of Franklin D. Roosevelt, but differed sharply in the types of programs enacted.

Some Great Society proposals were stalled initiatives from John F. Kennedy's New Frontier. Johnson's success depended on his skills of persuasion, coupled with the Democratic landslide in the 1964 election that brought in many new liberals to Congress, making the 1965 House of Representatives the most liberal House since 1938. Anti-war Democrats complained that spending on the Vietnam War choked off the Great Society. While some of the programs have been eliminated or had their funding reduced, many of them, including Medicare, Medicaid, the Older Americans Act and federal education funding, continue to the present. The Great Society's programs expanded under the administrations of Richard Nixon and Gerald Ford.

The New Deal, the New Frontier and the Great Society...

all with those feel good titles. Our government at work... working its way into every aspect of our lives...our very being. Always nurturing a co-dependent relationship with its constituency to ensure its re-election each cycle. As the populace becomes more and more dependent, the government becomes stronger and more controlling. An ever-growing segment of our general public seems to have reached a point where they depend on the government to not only think for them, but also to tell them how to live their lives.

Shortly after the New Year kicked-in, while reading from my local newspaper, I came across an article regarding new California legislation (760 new laws and/or mandates, give or take) for 2012.

Examples:

A ban on non-fitted sheets in motels.

Mandatory gay history for first-graders.

Car seats for children up to the age of 8.

California this week became the first state in the nation to make tanning beds off-limits to anyone younger than 18.

California chain restaurants will have to post calorie information on their menus and indoor menu boards.

Curiously, nearly every author of these brilliant laws had a "D" after their name. I can only guess that with the apparent absence of common sense parenting and self-regulating choices, our "nanny state" is just taking on the responsibility of guiding the mindless.

All this and the continuing insolvent jurisdiction that is,

year after year...causing more and more of its "productive class" to abandon the state. But not to worry, even as these personal-accountability advocates exit the state, California's population is increasing...fueled by the influx of illegal immigrants and California's entitlement culture.

The ultimate result of liberals seeking to shield the populace from the effects of its follies is to fill the world with fools.

In 1973, the draft ended and the United States converted to an all-volunteer military and the registration requirement was suspended in April 1975. President Carter resumed the registration function in 1980 in response to the Soviet invasion of Afghanistan. Registration continues today as a hedge against underestimating the number of servicemen needed in a future crisis.

It would be prudent to say the United States Military prefers not to have a military draft, as motivated volunteers are much more desirable than reluctant conscripts. Fortunately there are still enough patriotic Americans who are deciding to contribute to the War on Terror.

While no one wants to see his or her sons and/or daughters in harms way, the service seems to prepare them for the real world. The volunteer system is supported by our very best...with rural Americans carrying that heavy load disproportionately. These Americans are fighting for our country while too many others are living in a virtual world of video games and cell phone toys even as they're demanding more and more from America's entitlement culture.

I believe the elimination of the draft and the accompanying military training, has played a role in the decline of character, manners, discipline, patriotism, work ethic, physical condition and other common sense attributes in our younger generations.

After World War I the United States reduced the size of its military and got a costly wake-up call at Pearl Harbor. After World War II we cut the military back once again, and as before...we got another rude awakening. We were drawn into the Korean conflict, along with several other super powers, where we became combatants in a proxy war.

And now a president with zero military experience and no historical perspective is cutting our military back again (in favor of other domestic and international social programs...like funding Planned Parenthood and advocating homosexuality on the international stage), leaving us exposed to another...and probably even more devastating, wake-up call.

America's armed forces spend about 80 percent of their budgets "not on bullets and bombs" but on training and compensating our soldiers. Often, they do a far better job of shaping the minds and character of our youth than do our colleges. Somehow the military can take an 18-year old and teach him to park a 100 million dollar fighter across a carrier deck, but our colleges cannot even ensure that his civilian counterpart will show up regularly for classes. Young men and women leave the service debt-free and with marketable skills. Too many of our college students pile up debt and become increasingly angry that by their mid-20s...they still have received neither competitive skills nor a real education.

We have a raging obesity epidemic; tattoos and skin/body "piercings" are the trendy norm and our mindless citizenry's only outward concerns are wrapped around their continuous checking for...or returning text messages.

Almost one-half of our population is receiving some level of government welfare and/or assistance, but even those government dependents are well represented amongst the zombie texting taskforce. We're looking more and more like a deadbeat nation.

Our world is spinning out of control and most are oblivious to the impending peril.

The decline of past civilizations, (fourth-century-B.C., Athens...fifth-century-A.D., Rome...fifteenth-century, Byzantium or 1930s, Western Europe) was not caused by spending too much money on defense or not spending enough on public entitlements. Rather, their expanding governments redistributed more and more borrowed money, while a dependent citizenry wanted even fewer soldiers to guarantee ever more handouts.

History's bleak lesson is that those societies with self-reliant citizens who protect themselves and their interests...prosper; those who grow dependent cut back their defenses...and waste away.

Please bear with me now...because like Willie Nelson, I have a long list of real good reasons.

> "As democracy is perfected, the office of the President will represent, more and more closely, the inner soul of the people. On some great and glorious day the plain folks of the land will reach their heart's desire at last and the White House will be adorned by a downright moron."
>
> H.L. Mencken, The Baltimore Evening, Sunday, July 26, 1920

TABLE OF CONTENTS

CHAPTER 1

In the first month of his presidency, Obama avowed that if in three years he hadn't alleviated the nation's economic pain, he'd be a "one-term proposition."

But guess what? Obama is now saying he deserves re-election, despite the nation's continuing economic troubles.

He also said, "The country needs to return to old-fashioned American values so that everyone gets a fair shake."

The first question that comes to my mind is, "What does he know...or even care, about old-fashion American values?"

All Christians agreed with President Obama when he said, "The Bible calls us to help the poor." Yes, the Bible tells us that the poor you will always have with you, help them when you can. But Jesus was speaking to believers and not the government in his passage.

Like so many others, Obama selects only verse(s) that

support his socialist views. The Bible also says, "If a man who is capable does not work, he should not eat."

In one of the Ten Commandments we read, "Thou shalt not steal." It is wrong if I steal from someone who has more than me and it is equally as wrong if the government steals from me to give to someone else. Another commandment tells us not to covet our neighbor's possessions.

In his State of the Union address, President Barack Obama characterized the choice as one between whether "a shrinking number of people do really well while a growing number of Americans barely get by"...or his own vision, "where everyone gets a fair shot."

How ridiculous is that statement. Everyone who has ever been born in this country in the last 250 years has had a fair shot. It's what they did with that shot that made the difference and very few, if any, made it on socialist policies. The majority of a "shrinking number of people" as Obama puts it, started off poor as church mice and through plain old hard work and determination, became successful at whatever their dreams drove them to do and they did it without government interference or subsidy.

In a random cross section of American life in all categories such as politics, sports, music or pop culture, there is probably not one name that became wealthy on "leveling the playing field."

For instance, let's just pull a few names out of the hat:

The Kennedys got off the boat (legally) in the early 20th century to be met with scorn for their Irish heritage. Like all other Irish people of their day, they worked at low-level jobs before figuring out a way to rise up in their section of Boston and capture politics. The government didn't level their playing field.

Michael Jackson sure didn't start off as the "King of Pop." He was the eighth of 10 children in an African American working-class family who lived in a small three-room house in Gary, Indiana. He often said his father's strict discipline played a huge role in his success. The government didn't level his family's playing field.

Mickey Mantle came from Commerce, Oklahoma where his father worked in lead and zinc mines. After a brief slump in the majors, Mantle was given a stern message from his father that since baseball didn't seem to be working out for him, then maybe Mickey should return to Oklahoma and work in the mines with him. That alternative made Mantle immediately break out of his slump and he went on to become the highest paid active player of his time. The government didn't level his playing field.

Steve Jobs was born in San Francisco to two university students who were unmarried at the time...so he was adopted at birth. After high school graduation, Jobs enrolled at Reed College in Portland, Oregon where he dropped out after only one semester. However, he continued with auditing classes. Jobs credits his dropping in on a calligraphy course in college with the Mac's multiple typefaces or proportionally spaced fonts. He would go on and change the way we all communicate in this world. The government didn't level his playing field.

The point is that "fair shot" usually comes down to what kind of choices people make for themselves. If it's a lifetime of bad choices and laziness, then chances are that "fair shot" given to each American at birth is going to put them in the "growing number of Americans barely getting by."

When our country accepts Obama's suggestion to "level the playing field," what type of "creative/motivated people" will we have lost in the process? What will our children eventually turn into when working for success is not in style...of course it wouldn't be anything to be ashamed of if they decided to run for public office?

Entitlement is killing European countries, and it will have the same effect on this country unless Americans start cherishing and learning from those who have succeeded financially in our country and begin to apply it to their own situations...all without having the government leveling the playing field for them.

Critiquing the gospel of economic morality:

Obama keeps saying he wants the rich to pay their "fair" share. Obviously he chooses to spin the meaning of the word fair. Fair means free of bias, dishonesty and injustice.

"Bias" means to judge and then treat one group of people differently than others. The rationale for taxing higher wage earners at higher tax rates is due to a preconceived notion that high-income producers have less need for income than others. The idea is built on bias so it is unjust.

"Everyone should pay their fair share." I agree, but currently just under half of the people in this country do not pay any federal tax. I would like to meet someone who really thinks that "nothing" is the "fair share" for those Americans.

A more fundamental problem with the "fairness" issue is the slippery vagueness of the word "fair."

To ask whether life is fair...either here and now, or at any time or place around the world, over the past several thousand years...is to ask a rhetorical question. Life has seldom been within shouting distance of fair, in the sense of even approximately equal prospects of success for all.

Karl Marx first proposed progressive taxation in 1848. It followed his philosophy of "from each according to his ability, to each according to their needs." Marx believed... as Obama apparently does, that inequalities are immoral and that taxation is an appropriate means of reducing them. Therefore, the philosophical basis of higher-income tax rates on higher earners creates equality of outcomes.

However, morality is a system governing the selection of right and wrong with accountability for choices made. If all outcomes are the same, one's choices have no consequences, and there is no morality. A moral system is not one where an unemployed high school dropout is paid the same as a neurosurgeon.

Our republic was founded on the idea that all men are created equal and should receive equal treatment under the law. However, a higher income-tax rate for higher earners violates this principle. By taxing a higher income producer's earnings proportionally more, our tax system treats this property differently than other people's property, which implies that the property rights of the entrepreneurs, lawyers and university deans are not as sacred as the property rights of students, coffee shop workers, and dishwashers who earn less. It means the majority's property rights are superior to the rights of the minority. While the high-income producers may not be a sympathetic group, they, like criminals, should not be denied equal protection under the law.

So, while Obama preaches the moral superiority of tax increases on higher-income producers, consider this: He proposes a biased, unjust approach to social engineering.

He will penalize those who take risks, work hard and develop unique skills valued by our society. He sees no problem undermining high-income producers' property rights.

When three-quarters of Americans think the country is on the "wrong track" and even Bill Clinton called the economy "lousy," how then can Obama run for a second term?

Traveling to Osawatomie, Kansas, site of a famous 1910 Teddy Roosevelt speech, Obama laid out his case for a second term. Since he can't run on his record he has come up with another version of the "Hope and Change" illusion. It's now the even more abstract "Fairness" fantasy.

His recent pronouncement in Kansas tells me two things: One, his policies have failed, and two, it's not his fault. Shame on you, Mr. President.

When elected, if my memory serves me correctly...and I know it does, you declared that you...and you alone, would be accountable if your policies failed.

In 2008, many who agreed that he lacked executive qualifications nonetheless raved about Obama's oratory skills, intellect, and cool character. Those people...conservatives included, ought now to be deeply embarrassed. The man thinks and speaks in the hoariest of clichés, and that's when he has his teleprompter in front of him; when the prompter is absent he can barely think or speak at all. Not one original idea has ever issued forth from his mouth...it's all warmed-over Marxism of the kind that has failed over and over again for more than 100 years.

And what about his character? Obama is constantly

blaming anything and everything else for his troubles. Bush did it; it was bad luck; I inherited this mess. It is embarrassing to see a president so willing to advertise his own powerlessness and yet, so comfortable with his own incompetence. But really, what were we to expect? The man has never been responsible for anything, so how do we expect him to act responsibly?

In short: He is a small and small-minded man, with neither the temperament nor the intellect to handle his job. When you understand that, and only when you understand that, will the current erosion of liberty and prosperity make sense. It could not have gone otherwise with such a man in the Oval Office.

"What's frustrating people is that I've not been able to implement every aspect of what I said in 2008. *Well, it turns out that the Founders designed a system that makes it more difficult to bring about change than I would like sometimes.* But what we have been able to do is move in the right direction," Obama said.

I'm not surprised at his lack of meaningful accomplishments because I've never expected much real substance from him. His true agenda has always been a concern of mine...there's just an unsettling aura about the man. Everything he has done appears to be contrary to America's long-term continuance as the leader of the free world. I truly doubt that he has America's best interest in mind as he's looking ahead to a second term where he will not be encumbered by public opinion.

Barack Obama to Dmitry Medvedev (unaware of an open mic) on March 26, 2012:

"On all these issues, but particularly missile defense, this can be solved, but it's important for him (Putin) to give me space. This is 'my' last election. After 'my' election, I will have more flexibility."

"I will transmit this information to Vladimir," Medvedev assured Obama...adding, "I stand with you." A nice endorsement from Putin's puppet; it should be enough to chill friends and allies, democrats and dissidents, all over the world.

Americans were treated to an interesting exchange between President Barack Obama and Russian President Dmitry Medvedev. These two men, seated in close proximity, leaned into the other's personal space. They spoke in hushed tones, indicative of secret communication and nodded in agreement. In a rare display of affection between men, each patted the other's hands and arms.

In conversation not intended for the public, Obama told Medvedev that following his election he would be able to be more "flexible" about negotiations. These negotiations involve development and deployment of a missile defense system by the United States that the Russians strongly oppose.

Evaluation of the participants' body language and spoken words would lead even a casual observer to only one conclusion, which is that Obama has conspired to support the Russian position, while keeping his intent secret from the American people. Some might consider this conspiracy to commit treason. I do.

On which of "all these issues"...Syria, Iran, Eastern Europe, Georgia and/or human rights, is Obama ready to offer Putin yet more flexibility as soon as he gets past "his" last election? Where else will he show United States adversaries more flexibility? Yet more aid to North Korea? More weakening of tough Senate sanctions against Iran?

His message to Putin also implies he fully understands that such concessions would not be supported by the American people or Congress.

It is troubling that he suggested to Russian leaders that their reckless ambition would be rewarded with greater "flexibility" on our missile defense program after the upcoming election. It has significant implications for the security of our homeland, sends a terrible signal to our allies around the world, and calls into question the effectiveness of his "reset" policy with the Russian government. He is playing fast and loose with national security in my view...this should be an eye opener for "everyone" regarding a second Obama term as President of the United States.

Can you imagine the kind of pressure a re-elected Obama will put on Israel, the kind of anxiety he will induce from Georgia to the Persian Gulf, the nervousness among our most loyal East European friends who, having already once been left out on a limb by Obama, are now wondering what new flexibility Obama will show Putin... the man who famously proclaimed that the "greatest geopolitical upheaval" of the 20th century was Russia's loss of its Soviet empire. They didn't know. "We" didn't even know this was coming...until the mic was left open. Only Putin was to know.

In addressing this awkward situation one of Obama's minions...a talking head, said, "There are not too many things more buffoonish than suggesting the possibility of a treasonous post-election Obama." Well, I would agree that there aren't many, but the absolute certainty of a non-treasonous post-election Obama would be one of them. The best thing we can do to predict someone's future behavior is to listen...and then compare how their words match up with their past actions. Obama has previously stated what he thinks about nuclear weapons and what he intends to do in that regard. We only have to connect a few dots to know what's coming next.

> "The Constitution is not an instrument for the government to restrain the people; it is an instrument for the people to restrain the government...lest it come to dominate our lives and interests."
>
> Patrick Henry

CHAPTER 2

As children, we were told that we had a Constitutional Republic; as an adult, it was a Democracy, and now it's a Socialist nation. So what are we now? Well, I finally found out. I read about a new word for this year's edition of Urban Dictionary. The word and definition are as follows: Ineptocracy, (in-ept-oc-ra-cy); a system of government where the least capable to lead are elected by the least capable of producing, and where the members of society least likely to sustain themselves or succeed, are rewarded with goods and services paid for by the confiscated wealth of a diminishing number of producers.

There are times when our political system, whose essential job is to mediate conflicts in broadly acceptable and desirable ways, is simply not up to the task. It fails. This may be one of those times. What we learned in 2011 is that the frustrating and confusing budget debate may never reach a workable conclusion. It may continue indefinitely until it's abruptly ended by a severe economic or financial crisis that wrenches control from elected leaders.

We are shifting from "give away politics" to "take away

politics." Since World War II, presidents and Congresses have been in the enviable position of distributing more benefits to more people without requiring ever-steeper taxes. Now, this governing formula no longer works, and politicians face the opposite, taking away... reducing benefits or raising taxes significantly, to prevent government deficits from destabilizing the economy. It is not clear whether either Democrats or Republicans can navigate the change.

Our political system has failed before. Conflicts that could not be resolved through debate, compromise and legislation were settled in more primitive and violent ways. The Civil War was the greatest and most tragic failure; leaders couldn't end slavery peacefully. In our time, the social protests and disorders of the 1960s...the civil rights and anti-war movements and urban riots... almost overwhelmed the political process. So did double-digit inflation, peaking at 13 percent in 1979 and 1980, which for years defied efforts to control it.

The budget impasse raises comparable questions. Can we resolve it before some ill-defined crisis imposes its own terms? For years, there has been a "something for nothing" aspect to our politics. More people became dependent on government. From 1960 to 2010, the share of federal spending going for "payments to individuals" (Social Security, food stamps, Medicare and the like) climbed from 26 percent to 66 percent. Meanwhile, the tax burden barely budged. In 1960, federal taxes were 17.8 percent of the national income (gross domestic product). In 2007, they were 18.5 percent of GDP.

This good fortune reflected falling military spending... from 52 percent of federal outlays in 1960 to 20 percent today...and solid economic growth that produced ample tax revenues. Generally modest budget deficits bridged any gap. But now this favorable arithmetic has collapsed under the weight of slower economic growth (even after a recovery from the recession), an aging population (increasing the number of recipients) and high health costs (already 26 percent of federal spending). Present and prospective deficits are gargantuan.

The trouble is, that while the economics of give away policies have changed, the politics haven't. Liberals still want more spending and conservatives more tax cuts. (Although the tax burden has stayed steady, various "cuts" have offset projected increases and shifted the burden.) With a few exceptions, Democrats and Republicans haven't embraced detailed take away policies to reconcile America's appetite for government benefits with its distaste for taxes. Obama has provided no leadership. And aside from Paul Ryan, chairman of the House Budget Committee, few Republicans have stepped forward.

No one wants to take away; it's more fun to give. All 2011's budget feuds...over the debt ceiling, the super committee, the payroll tax cut, skirted the central issues. There's a legitimate debate about how fast deficits should be reduced to avoid jeopardizing the economic recovery, notes Charles Blahous, a White House official in the George W. Bush Administration. But the long-term budget problem, as he says, stems from Social Security, Medicare and other health programs.

Any resolution of the budget impasse must repudiate, at least partially, the past half-century's politics. Conservatives look at the required tax increases and say, "No way." Liberals look at the required benefit cuts and say, "No way."

Each reverts to scripted evasions. Liberals imply (wrongly) that taxing the rich will solve the long-term budget problem. It won't. For example, the Forbes 400 richest

Americans have a collective wealth of $1.5 trillion. If the government simply confiscated everything they own, and turned them into paupers, it would barely cover the one-time 2011 deficit increase of $1.3 trillion. Conservatives deplore "spending" in the abstract, ignoring the popularity of much spending, especially for Social Security and Medicare.

So the political system is failing. It's stuck in the past. It's unwilling to make the necessary choices regarding America's long-term viability. It's unwilling to resolve the deep conflicts.

Politicians of both parties have addicted much of the public to government spending with an ever-increasing array of entitlements. Like an addict who goes through his bank account, "maxes" out his credit cards and finally pawns his possessions, our society is on the brink of a fatal overdose. Yet our leaders seem simply unwilling to face this addiction; they are the pushers making it worse. One could argue that too many of our leaders are addicted to the power they get from passing the spending policies that are killing our society.

How bad is it? Our nation will be over 16 trillion dollars in debt if Obama gets his latest debt-ceiling increase. In numbers it looks like this: $16,000,000,000,000

Even writing it out in zeros doesn't give you a real perspective about how much 16 trillion really is.

It's the "and counting" part that is even more frightening. This year's federal budget deficit alone is more than $1 trillion. Even if the congressional super committee had been able to come up with the ballyhooed $1.2 trillion in proposed cuts, those savings would have been stretched out over 10 years. At best, this would only slow down the rate of increase in the debt, and that would only happen if the promised cuts were actually enacted...which is always questionable down the road.

Public debt has increased by 67 percent over the past three years, and too many Americans refuse even to see that as a problem. And...there is no politically plausible scenario under which the $16.4 trillion will be reduced to $13.2 trillion, and then $6.9 trillion and, eventually, balanced. At the deepest echelons of our governing structures, they are committed to living beyond our means on a scale no civilization has ever done...and survived.

In a mere half-century, the richest nation on Earth has become the most mortgaged nation in the history of the world; while the attitudes and assumptions of half the population and most of our governing elitists have remained unchanged.

Currently, it would take $48,000 from each and every citizen in the United States to pay off our debt. But... guess what? For us taxpayers (the only ones paying), our share of the debt is more than $133,000 each. And this does not count the un-funded liabilities of social programs we are committed to meet.

Why is the looming disaster that should be obvious to our elected leaders being ignored by all of them except for the incoming Tea Party Republicans and a few libertarians, like Ron Paul? The only reasonable answer seems to be fear of angering an electorate accustomed to government handouts and too shortsighted to understand the inevitable consequences of unsustainable spending. Those receiving entitlements, like people who smoke or drink, know it isn't good for them, yet believe there is still time to change, "someday." The reality is that the public addiction to spending for entitlements has grown to become much like a very serious drug habit, the kind that can kill the addict...and/or destroy our society.

An alternative theory is that we're muddling our way to a messy consensus. All the studies and failed negotiations are laying the groundwork for an eventual accommodation. Perhaps. But it's just as likely that this year's partisan "scapegoating" implies more partisan "scapegoating." Political leaders assume that financial markets won't ever choke on the United States' debt and force higher interest rates, stiff spending cuts and tax increases.

At best, this is wishful thinking. At worst, it's playing Russian roulette with the country's future.

But the real, unacknowledged problem today is that the people who vote for a living outnumber the people who work for a living.

I am reminded that Benjamin Franklin correctly saw our nation's destiny when he said, "When the people find that they can vote themselves money, that will herald the end of the republic."

> "A long habit of not thinking a thing wrong gives it a superficial appearance of being right."
> Thomas Paine

CHAPTER 3

I n 1933, President-elect Franklin D. Roosevelt escaped an assassination attempt in Miami that mortally wounded Chicago Mayor Anton J. Cermak; the gunman, Giuseppe Zangara, was summarily executed a month later.

Yes, it took the justice system only one month to do its job in ridding the community of a violent member of society. But today...less than 90 years later, justice is so hampered by our liberal/progressive culture that criminals like Giuseppe Zangara will...in most cases, never pay the full price for their crimes. The courts have become so muddled with seemingly unending appeals that drag on for years and years. And as for the death penalty cases...the odds are that the individual will die of natural causes before any execution is mandated. And even if they spend the rest of their lives in prison, prisons today are a far cry from what prisons were originally intended to be.

Driven by an ever-expanding liberal/progressive culture, our criminal system has become just another mutation of what common sense used to look like...before the all-encompassing equalizer: "It's not my fault; It's not his or her fault; It's not their fault"; the problems must stem from their environment, our culture, a dysfunctional family; lack of a formal education, and of course the always affective "race card"...anything but personal responsibility and accountability.

Researcher and author, James Q. Wilson's analysis of crime, and the effect of criminal law, have debunked the theories of many intellectuals, who had led judges and legislators to ease up on criminals...leading the way to skyrocketing rates of crime, including murder.

Prior to 1960, murder rates in the United States had been going down for decades. Even the absolute number of murders declined, while the population grew by millions...despite the addition of two new states, Hawaii and Alaska. In 1960, the number of murders in the 50 states was less than it had been in the 48 states 30 years earlier.

The murder rate in 1960 was just under half of what it had been in 1934.

But that was not good enough for the intelligentsia, with their theories on how to "solve" our "problems." First of all, they claimed, we had to stop focusing on punishment and get at the "root causes" of crime. In other words, we had to solve the criminals' problems, in order to solve the problem of crime.

This approach was not new in the 1960s. In fact, it went back at least as far as the 18th century. But what was new in the 1960s was the widespread acceptance of such notions in the legal system, including the Supreme Court of the United States.

The crusade against punishment, and especially capital punishment, spread through all three branches of the federal government and into state governments as well. Even a murderer caught in the act had so many new "rights," created out of thin air by judges, that executing him could require a decade or more of additional litigation, even after he was found guilty.

The best-known product of this 1960s revolution in the criminal law was the famous Miranda warning, "You have the right to remain silent," etc. It is as if we are engaged in some kind of sporting contest with the criminal, and must give him a chance to beat the rap, even when he is guilty.

In the aftermath of this revolution in criminal law, promoted by the intelligentsia in academia and in the media, the long downward trend in murder suddenly reversed. By 1974, the murder rate was more than twice what it had been in 1961. Between 1960 and 1976, a citizen's chances of becoming a victim of a major violent crime tripled. So did the murder of policemen.

People clever with words sought all sorts of ways of denying the obvious fact that the fancy new developments in criminal law were catastrophically counterproductive. But eventually reality surfaced...driven by research and ever-rising numbers, cutting through all the fancy evasions with hard facts and hard logic.

The idea that crime results from poverty, or can be reduced by alleviating poverty, was shot down by pointing out that crime rose the fastest in this country at a time when the number of people living in poverty or squalor was declining. Wilson said, "I have yet to see a 'root cause' or to encounter a government program that has successfully attacked it." Nor did Wilson buy the argument that unemployment drove people to crime or welfare. He noted that, "the work force was at an all-time high at the same time as were the welfare rolls." Nor were minorities frozen out of this economy. By 1969, "the nonwhite unemployment rate had fallen to 6.5 percent," he pointed out.

By systematically confronting the prevailing notions and rhetoric with undeniable facts to the contrary, Wilson began to wear away the prevailing social dogmas of intellectuals behind the counterproductive changes in law and society.

The common sense that had once produced and sustained declining crime rates began to reappear, here and there, in the criminal justice system and sometimes prevailed. Murder rates began to decline again. James Q. Wilson was the leader in this fight. He said, "We have trifled with the wicked."

In spite of some small incremental improvements in dealing with our criminal elements, they still hold a lot of cards...and the wild card (life hasn't been fair) is always in play.

Of course being in one of America's prisons today is a far cry from the "hard time" prisons of the past when we had work details, chain gangs and solitary confinement. Today's prisons (except maybe for Arizona's Sheriff Joe Arpaio's prison) have taken on the appearance of gated retirement communities with exercise facilities, libraries, televisions and community centers for prisoners and visitors.

My favorite folly regarding how our government deals with the criminal element is the force-feeding of inmates when they go on hunger strikes to get policies and regulations changed in our prison systems. I recently read where gang members in several different California (of course) prisons went on a hunger strike because the prison's policies didn't allow them certain liberties.

The courts have actually ruled that prisoners engaging in hunger strikes may be force-fed. In cases where an entity (usually the state) has or is able to obtain custody of the hunger striker (such as a prisoner), the hunger strike is often terminated by the custodial entity through the use of force-feeding.

"Prisons may force-feed inmates on hunger strikes because the state's obligation to protect the health of its citizens trumps the prisoner's right to make medical choices, an appellate court has ruled."

I guess it's just me, but I've never understood how a hunger strike works...just always thought if their bluff was called...and they got hungry enough, they'd eat.

> "If you want total security, go to prison. There you're fed, clothed, given medical care, housing and so on. The only thing lacking... is freedom."
> Dwight D. Eisenhower

CHAPTER 4

Personal debt is the worst drug in America, because it directly harms the most people.

The debt pushers have enlisted builders, retailers and real estate agents to sing their siren songs of "buy now, pay later" and "buy more and bigger with credit." Despite the current economic disaster, some still push the dangerous idea of creating wealth by using other people's money. We'll be happier and stronger when we finally shun the debt-pushers and move to a wealth-centered culture.

Buy a $500 washing machine on a credit card and make minimum payments, and it turns into a $1,000 washing machine. It can make someone who should be a happy real estate investor, homeowner or car owner into a worried mess, barely able to make payments and hoping nothing goes wrong. Just as with illegal drugs, the temporary happiness it promises is a fleeting illusion, quickly replaced by a grim reality. Economic downturns should be buying opportunities that help build wealth, but for those who are in debt they are times when their dreams and wealth are destroyed.

Our debt-centered culture has even caused us to corrupt

our language. Someone with less than 100 percent equity in a car, house, apartment building, or office tower is not simply an owner. They are a co-owner. If a person has less than 50 percent equity, he or she is a minor co-owner. In a wealth-centered culture, we'd use the right words, and strive to be owners, not minor co-owners.

It is sad that so many of us have yet to know the joy and freedom of being debt-free. Buying new cars with cash is great fun, as the dealer personnel just do not believe it until you hand them the check. Paying-off a home is cause for celebration. Buying investment properties with cash is still more fun.

There is no caste system, royalty or other impediments in the United States to prevent anyone from building wealth by studying hard, working hard, working smart, saving and investing.

Many people who fancy themselves as sophisticated real estate investors are really just rent collectors for banks, stuck with almost all of the risk and little of the reward. If a tenant sues an apartment "owner" because their child was poisoned by lead-based paint, the bank has almost zero risk, but the "owner" can lose everything. A commercial property "owner" who needs cash at a time when prices are down may lose equity when the property is sold, yet the bank loan still needs to be paid in full.

Using other people's money is still touted by some as wise and the way to true wealth, but it is really just gambling. Another word for using borrowed money is "leverage." Like any lever, it can exert force in two directions, upending the investor/gambler's best-laid schemes. A vacancy in a rental property owned outright is nothing more than an inconvenience. A vacancy of a highly leveraged property often causes great distress and collapse of an economic house of cards.

Anticipating appreciation, some argue that now is an excellent time to use loans to buy four times as much investment property as could be purchased with cash (25 percent down on each). The overall net rent might be about the same, yet the appreciation would be four times as great. As with anything which sounds too good to be true, the risks are many. A vacancy means negative cash flow. Four times as many properties mean four times the liability. Maintenance expenses are four times as much. Using loans is actually a gamble that nothing will go wrong and that there will be significant appreciation.

Easy credit has prompted homebuilders to make ever larger and fancier houses, and carmakers to make larger and fancier vehicles. Both promise an increase in happiness commensurate with the increase in size and features. But, who is inside? A happy owner with no worries about payments or a debtor struggling to make payments?

Excessive houses and cars waste energy and materials, and require more maintenance. Waste is not virtuous. An oversize house often leads to more debt, as "owners" overheat credit cards and efforts to fill all the space. Drastic reductions in sales of cars and houses mean we have reached the point where even sellers and lenders no longer benefit from the excesses.

Despite the class-warfare rhetoric of leftist politicians and the garish lifestyles of some celebrities, most wealthy people in the United States are not showoffs. They do not need or want extravagant cars, wristwatches, houses, clothing and so forth.

The best-selling book, "The Millionaire Next Door," by Thomas J. Stanley and William D. Danko, and Stanley's subsequent books, are entertaining to read as they demolish leftist myths about those who are wealthy. They should be used as textbooks in every high school, and every school should have personal financial management classes.

We've got to stop putting the debt-pushers at the center of our economy and lives. Debt-slavery destroys dreams and opportunities, impoverishing our nation and our society. It is no wonder that politicians wildly overspend, as they are part of a nation that has been wildly overspending for many decades.

Rejecting the culture of debt and embracing a culture of wealth will return us to the happiness and freedom, which are our birthright.

After reading about Paris Hilton's $300,000 Christmas gift (a California Spyder Ferrari) to herself...her second luxury car, I received an epiphany about a large part of the 21st Century's troubling issues. There are entirely too many toys available to...and coveted by, the post-1950s generations of Americans:

As observed at the various Occupy Wall Street demonstrations, "I want it, and I want it now"...or there will be a tantrum!

But most of the above mindless antics are just the superficial symptoms of a reoccurring phenomenon driven by governmental intervention in the arena of economics. *"Central planning..."*

Skimming through decades of news, testimony and arcane trade reports, I'm reminded that this has happened before, and that there was nothing secret about the public and/or business decisions that led to cheap money, price inflation, collapse, mass foreclosures and bailouts.

Americans' refusal to worry too much about history is a

national strength in some ways, but it also makes our recurring financial crises more emphatic.

In the early Republic, borrowed money was for rich people only; for everyone else, it was a sign of weakness and impending doom. Speculators, gamblers and other marginal figures who gave in to their weaknesses and borrowed were liable to wind up in debtors' jails.

Fannie Mae and Freddie Mac pushed home-loan finance costs down when they started large-scale home-loan sales through Wall Street banks. Credit card and student lenders did also. Home prices and consumer debt were soon rising far more rapidly than worker incomes. But since homeowners were worth more, on paper, every year, the new debt seemed to get absorbed, until it didn't, and the economy froze.

"We're currently in the "eye of the storm." The nation is still heavily leveraged. The economy could grind to a halt again when interest rates finally start rising; and the payments on those low *variable-rate* loans start ramping up...and once again, overwhelm borrowers. Another bubble?

I'm forced to suggest that much of the above self-indulgence was...and continues to be driven by the commercialization of the phrase..."You deserve it!" And of course that logic would later spawn yet another self-serving declaration, "It's not your fault"...that your house is in foreclosure.

It just seems to be the prevailing policy in America today, as we hear it a lot from the White House: "It's not my fault."

Why is living within ones means such a difficult concept

to comprehend? Shouldn't we all know by now that we need to "pay to play?"

Growing up in Arkansas, during the 40s and 50s, I was informed over and over again, that if we couldn't pay cash for an item(s)...we could probably live without it.

CHAPTER 5

Oakland California:

Police arrested about 300 people Saturday as Occupy Oakland protesters spent a portion of their day trying to get inside a vacant convention center before moving on with plans to occupy a local YMCA...but with failures at both locations, they broke into City Hall.

Mayor Jean Quan said, "Protestors forced their way into City Hall, where they 'burned an American flag,' broke into an electrical box and damaged art structures."

I wouldn't think it would be worthwhile to draw attention to the Occupy Wall Street "movement," or its list of demands that wouldn't pass muster in an average kindergarten class.

But if America's president and vice president choose to talk about it, and give it credibility, then it's news.

According to Vice President Joe Biden, demands such as free college, pay independent of work, a $20 minimum wage (Why not $100?), and a nation with open borders have legitimacy and "a lot in common with the Tea Party movement."

This should provide perspective to what our most fundamental problem is today. We have an endangered species in America whose loss threatens our future. That species is called the American adult.

Can someone please explain to our vice president the difference between a screaming infant not getting what he or she wants...when he or she wants it, and an adult who understands personal responsibility, humility, work and service to others?

A functioning free society requires citizens who are adults, capable of overseeing and administering a government that enforces laws that protect life and property.

Once our government became a playpen for those who believe they run the universe and make its basic laws, and also believe that the rest of us must submit to their hallucinations about what is just, we wind up where we are today.

The Wall Street Journal reported recently that, according to the latest census data, 48.5 percent of American families are on the receiving end of some sort of government program, the highest percentage in our history.

To provide some perspective, this figure was 10 percent in the 1920s, and a little more than 30 percent in 1980. During the 1960s, a watershed decade when the infantile culture of narcissism began to permeate the free adult culture in America, more government programs were born than in any other period.

By 1980, four of these programs of the 1960s...food stamps, Pell grants, Medicare and Medicaid...accounted for $164 billion in annual spending. Today these four programs swallow almost an additional trillion dollars.

In all our history, there is only one instance of major reform of a government-spending program, and that was the welfare reform that was passed in 1996.

These government programs are pure monopolies driven by political power, not by efficiency or whether they are serving the real needs of citizens. They don't change... they only grow.

This contrasts with America's corporations, which Wall Street protestors on the Brooklyn Bridge, and America's president and vice president, would like us to believe control everything.

If big corporations did control everything, they would, like government programs, never change or lose power. But large firms regularly come and go, because, in contrast to government programs, they remain powerful only as long as they are serving consumers.

Of the 30 major corporations that constitute the Dow Jones Industrial Average firms, only eight were on the list in 1980. The 30 Dow Jones Industrial Average firms have changed 45 times since the average was started 115 years ago.

No, Mr. Biden...Occupy Wall Street has nothing in common with the Tea Party movement. The Tea Party movement is a protest against abuse of political power. Occupy Wall Street is about lust for political power.

President Obama has also given the Occupy Wall Street protesters his support and blessing, they seem to share basic opinions. Both believe that corporations are evil and Mr. Obama has made a specific point that corporations, or at least banks, do not have the right to make a profit from services provided to its customers, the "middle class."

Karl Marx, author of The Communist Manifesto, was extremely critical of the capitalist profit motive, railed against the wealthy that he called the "bourgeoisie" and believed that society should be a classless community and that the underprivileged should carry out organized action to bring about change.

I'm not privy to Mr. Obama's true philosophy, but if it walks like a duck, quacks like a duck...?

The Occupy Wall Street protesters don't want to end crony capitalism, with its handouts and government favoritism; they just want to be invited to the party.

Maybe it's just me, but I can't look at the Occupy Wall Street protesters without thinking, "Who parented these people?"

I have commented on the social and political ramifications of the "movement"...now known as "OWS"; but their utopian, fairyland agenda can be summarized by one of their placards: "Everything for everybody."

Thanks to their pipe-dream platform, it's clear there are "people" out there with serious designs on "transformational" change in America who are using the protesters like bed springs in a brothel.

Yet it's not my role as a writer that prompts my parenting question, but rather the fact that I'm the father of three adults. There are some crucial life lessons that the protesters' parents clearly have not passed along.

Here, then, are seven things the OWS protesters' parents

should have taught their children but obviously didn't, so I will:

> Life isn't fair. The concept of justice, that everyone should be treated fairly…is a worthy and worthwhile moral imperative on which our nation was founded. But justice and economic equality are not the same. Or, as Mick Jagger said, "You can't always get what you want."

> No matter how you try to "level the playing field," some people have better luck, skills, talents or connections that land them in better places. Some seem to have all the advantages in life but squander them, others play the modest hand they're dealt and make up the difference in hard work and perseverance, and some find jobs on Wall Street and eventually buy houses in the Hamptons. Is it fair? Stupid question…

> Nothing is "free." Protesting with signs that seek "free" college degrees and "free" health care make you look like idiots, because colleges and hospitals don't operate on rainbows and sunshine. There is no magic money machine to tap for your meandering educational careers and "slow paths" to adulthood, and the 53 percent of taxpaying Americans owe you neither a degree nor an annual physical.

> While I'm pointing out this obvious fact, here are a few other things that are not free: Overtime for police officers and municipal workers, trash hauling, repairs to fixtures and property, condoms, Band-Aids and the food that inexplicably appears on the tables in your makeshift protest kitchens. Real people with real dollars are underwriting your civic temper tantrum.

➢ Your word is your bond. When you demonstrate to eliminate student loan debt, you are advocating precisely the lack of integrity you decry in others. Loans are made based on solemn promises to repay them. No one forces you to borrow money; you are free to choose educational pursuits that don't require loans, or to seek technical or vocational training that allows you to support yourself and your ongoing educational goals. Also, for the record, being a college student is not a state of victimization. It's a privilege that billions of young people around the globe would die for...literally.

➢ A protest is not a party. The other day, on the Internet, I saw what isn't usually evident in the liberal media's newsreel footage of your demonstrations: Most of you are doing this only for attention and fun. Serious people in a sober pursuit of social and political change don't dance jigs down Sixth Avenue like attendees of a Renaissance festival. You look foolish, you smell gross, you are clearly high on something and you don't seem to realize that all around you are people who deem you irrelevant.

➢ There are reasons you haven't found jobs. The truth? Your tattooed necks, gauged ears, facial "piercings" and dirty dreadlocks are off-putting. Nonconformity for the sake of nonconformity isn't a virtue. Occupy reality: Only 4 percent of college graduates are out of work. If you are among that 4 percent, find a mirror and face the problem. It's not them. It's you.

Populist political movements are easily manipulated, often playing on class envy and covetousness. So, it might be interesting to see who the self-described 99-percenters are railing against.

Who is backing those 99-percenters, anyway?

In October, the protesters staged a "millionaires march" in New York City, parading to the homes of wealthy citizens such as Rupert Murdoch and David Koch. But only some riches bother the Occupiers, who have ignored the massive wealth of celebrities in their own ranks.

The top 25 richest celebrities supporting Occupy Wall Street, according to the website Celebrity Net Worth, possess a combined net worth just over $4 billion.

While JP Morgan and Chase banker Jamie Dimon's $200 million was a target of the millionaires march, he has a net worth less than five of the celebrities supporting OWS.

The top 14 supporters of OWS by wealth:

1. Yoko Ono, $500 million
2. Jay-Z, $450 million
3. David Letterman, $400 million
4. Stephen King, $400 million
5. Russell Simmons, $325 million
6. Sean Lennon, $200 million
7. Mike Myers, $175 million
8. George Clooney, $160 million.
9. Brad Pitt, $150 million
10. Don King, $150 million
11. Roger Waters (Pink Floyd), $145 million
12. Jane Fonda, $120 million
13. Miley Cyrus, 120 million
14. Al Gore, $100 million

I suspect the global warming profiteer Gore is worth substantially more. But here's the part I find so deliciously delightful. Funny woman Roseann Barr, that champion of the 99 percent, says:

"I do say that I am in favor of the return of the guillotine and that is for the worst of the worst of the guilty. I would first allow the guilty bankers to pay, you know, the ability to pay back anything over $100 million of personal wealth because I believe in a maximum wage of $100 million. And if they are unable to live on that amount then they should, you know, go to the re-education camps and if that doesn't help, then behead them."

Isn't it fascinating that Barr's estimated worth is $80 million. Under her plan, at least she'd keep her head... and bag of millions. It's always the other guy who has too much, isn't it?

Oh yeah, one other point. How much is George Soros worth? You know, the guy who is so sympathetic to the Occupy movement.

Government is the great fiction, through which everybody endeavors to live at the expense of everybody else.

> "Self-deceit, this fatal weakness of mankind, is the source of half the disorders of human life."
>
> Adam Smith

CHAPTER 6

B ut let's get back to the personal debt problems of
America's "I want it and I want it now" culture. I, of
course, would be the first to say, "They made their bed
and now they must sleep in it." They're "wanting" more
and more...bigger and better...even waiting in lines to
get the latest, high-priced, techno toy to replace the one
that's already obsolete. They haven't finished paying for
their existing "latest, greatest, gotta-have-plaything" that
they bought less than a year earlier. But not to worry,
they can just add the cost of their new, up-to-the-minute
model to the unpaid balance of their now obsolete status
symbol.

It's always about the latest techno gadgets, trendy styles
and being current in today's superficial...circus-midway
like world. However, I must admit there are extenuating
influences at work that are drivers for this craziness.
While these drivers are subliminally built-in to the very
fabric of our culture...I still believe in the power of free
choice.

In my preceding book I touched on the need for not
only America's economy to always be growing, but for
the entire world's economy to also constantly be moving

forward. But given the direction of this book, a deeper understanding of things that have contributed to the financial woes of America's individuals...and thereby affecting America's financial situation. The domino effect...

We've all said...at one time or another, "It seems like things always break down right after the warranty expires." And how many times have you been told by a service tech (when taking electronic items in for repair, after the warranty has run out) that it's cheaper to replace your printer, computer and/or whatever other electronics, than it is to repair it. Hence, the term..."a throwaway culture."

Planned obsolescence: If I didn't know better, I would say, "Sounds like another conspiracy theory to me." But guess what...?

Planned obsolescence or built-in obsolescence in industrial design is a policy of deliberately planning or designing a product with a limited useful life, so it will become obsolete or nonfunctional after a certain period of time. Planned obsolescence has potential benefits for a producer because to obtain continuing use of the product the consumer is under pressure to purchase again, whether from the same manufacturer (a replacement part or a newer model), or from a competitor which might also rely on planned obsolescence.

In some cases, deliberate deprecation of earlier versions of a technology is used to reduce ongoing support costs, especially in the software industry. Though this could be considered planned obsolescence, it differs from the classic form in that the consumer is typically made aware of the limited support lifetime of the product as part of their licensing agreement.

For an industry, planned obsolescence stimulates demand by encouraging purchasers to buy sooner if they still want a functioning product. Built-in obsolescence is used in many different products. There is, however, the potential backlash of consumers who learn that the manufacturer invested money to make the product obsolete faster; such consumers might turn to a producer (if any exists) that offers a more durable alternative.

Planned obsolescence was first developed in the 1920s and 1930s when mass production opened every single aspect of the production process to exacting analysis.

Estimates of planned obsolescence can influence a company's decisions about product engineering. Therefore the company can use the least expensive components that satisfy product lifetime projections. Such decisions are part of a broader discipline known as value engineering.

Origins of planned obsolescence go back at least as far as 1932 with Bernard London's pamphlet "Ending the Depression Through Planned Obsolescence." However, Brooks Stevens, an American industrial designer, first popularized the phrase in 1954. Stevens was due to give a talk at an advertising conference in Minneapolis, where without giving it much thought, used the term as the title of his seminar.

From that point on, "planned obsolescence" became Stevens' catchphrase. By his definition, planned obsolescence was "instilling in the buyers the desire to own something a little newer, a little better, a little sooner than is necessary." Others quickly picked up the term, but Stevens' definition would be challenged later.

By the late 1950s, planned obsolescence had become a commonly used term for products designed to break easily or to quickly go out of style. In fact, the concept was so widely recognized that in 1959, Volkswagen mocked it in a now-legendary advertising campaign. While acknowledging the widespread use of planned obsolescence among automobile manufacturers, Volkswagen pitched itself as an alternative. "We do not believe in planned obsolescence," the ads suggested. "We don't change a car for the sake of change."

In 1960, cultural critic Vance Packard published "The Waste Makers," promoted as an exposé of *"the systematic attempt of business to make us wasteful, debt-ridden, permanently discontented individuals."*

Packard divided planned obsolescence into two sub-categories: "Obsolescence of desirability" and "Obsolescence of function." Obsolescence of desirability, also called "psychological obsolescence," referred to marketers' attempts to wear out a product in the owner's mind. Packard quoted industrial designer George Nelson, who wrote: "Design is an attempt to make a contribution through change. When no contribution is made or can be made, the only process available for giving the illusion of change is styling!"

Technical or functional obsolescence: The design of most consumer products includes an expected average lifetime permeating all stages of development. Thus, it must be decided early in the design of a complex product how long it is designed to last so that each component can be made to those specifications.

Planned obsolescence is made more likely by making the cost of repairs comparable to the replacement cost, or by refusing to provide service or parts any longer. Some products may never have been serviceable. Creating new lines of products that do not interoperate with older products can also make an older model quickly obsolete, forcing replacement.

Planned functional obsolescence is a type of technical obsolescence in which companies introduce new technology that replaces the old. The old products do not have the same capabilities or functionality as the new ones.

Systemic obsolescence: Planned systemic obsolescence is the deliberate attempt to make a product obsolete by altering the system in which it is used in such a way as to make its continued use difficult. New software is frequently introduced that is not compatible with older software. This makes the older software largely obsolete. Even though an older version of a word processing program is operating correctly, it might not be able to read data saved by newer versions. The lack of interoperability forces many users to purchase new programs prematurely. The greater the network externalities in the market, the more effective this strategy is. Oftentimes, developers of hardware will try to prevent a product from being backwards compatible with older interchangeable cartridges and proprietary connector plugs.

Another way of introducing systemic obsolescence is to eliminate service and maintenance for a product. If a product fails, the user is forced to purchase a new one. This strategy seldom works because there are typically third parties that are prepared to perform the service if parts are still available.

Style obsolescence: Marketing may be driven primarily by aesthetic design. Product categories in this case display a fashion cycle. By continually introducing new designs, and retargeting or discontinuing others, a manufacturer can "ride the fashion cycle." Such product categories include the almost entirely style-driven clothing industry (riding the fashion cycle) and the mobile phone industries with constant minor feature enhancements and restyling.

Planned style obsolescence occurs when marketers change the styling of products so customers will purchase products more frequently. The style changes are designed to make owners of the old model feel "out of date." It is also designed to differentiate the product from the competition, thereby reducing price competition. One example of style obsolescence is the automobile industry, in which manufacturers typically make style changes every year or two. As the former CEO of General Motors, Alfred P. Sloan stated in 1941, "Today the appearance of a motorcar is the most important factor in the selling end of the business...because everyone knows that car will run."

Another strategy is to take advantage of fashion changes, often called the fashion cycle. The fashion cycle is the repeated introduction, rise, popular culmination, and decline of a style as it progresses through various social strata. Marketers can ride the fashion cycle by changing the mix of products that they direct at various market segments. This is very common in the clothing industry. A certain style of dress will initially be aimed at a very high-income segment, and then gradually be re-targeted to lower income segments. The fashion cycle can repeat itself, in which case a stylistically obsolete product may regain popularity and cease to be obsolete.

Notification obsolescence: Some companies have developed a version of obsolescence in which the product informs the user when it is time to buy a replacement. Examples of this include water filters that display a replacement notice after a predefined time and disposable razors that have a strip that changes color. Whether the user is notified before the product has actually deteriorated or the product simply deteriorates more quickly than is necessary, planned obsolescence is the result. In this way planned obsolescence may be introduced without the company going to the expense of developing a more "up to date" replacement model.

In some cases, notification may be combined with the deliberate disabling of a product to prevent it from working, thus requiring the buyer to purchase a replacement. Inkjet printer manufacturers who employ proprietary smart chips in their ink cartridges to prevent them from being used after a certain threshold (number of pages, time, etc.), even though the cartridge(s) may still contain usable ink or could be refilled (this is exactly what happened to my perfectly functioning Epson...it still went through all the motions of printing, but did not print). Some medical equipment also exploits this technique to ensure a steady stream of revenue from sales of replacement consumables. This constitutes programmed obsolescence, in that there is no random component to the decline in function.

Obsolescence by depletion: When a product consumes a resource, as when a computer printer consumes ink and paper, it is generally understood that this is unavoidable. But some products also consume related resources that need not be consumed. For example, a 4-color inkjet printer that is used mostly for printing in gray scale and seldom in color, may be pre-programmed to siphon off color inks even while printing black, so that the color cartridges must be replaced about the same time as the black ink cartridge (my Epson had been doing this all along before its smart chip triggered the complete shutdown).

Even the processed foods and beverages we routinely purchase everyday have "hurry-up and use" dates on them: "Sell by dates," "Best if used by dates" and my Bud Light has a "Born on date," while our pharmaceutical companies prefer the "Discard after date." But make no mistake, they're all about planting a subliminal message in your mind, "You need to hurry and use this product before it goes bad."

Home canned peaches were one of my mother's favorites and I have such fond memories of them from my childhood. We never had an "Eat by date" on them but I believe they had a "Canned date" on them...for mother's reference later. We never had so much in our home that someone needed to tell us to eat a certain item before it went bad. In those days we understood and appreciated what we had...wastefulness or extravagance was never a part of who we were.

Remember the days when a washing machine lasted for decades? And if it did break down...it could be fixed. But now it seems it is cheaper to discard our broken products and buy new ones. The side effects of our throwaway society are that we, as consumers, are spending more and more just to maintain our status quo, even as we're feeding those ever-growing waste mountains festering with toxic chemicals. This profit-driven market ploy is escalating the depletion of our natural resources such as rare metals.

There is much more at work in the marketplace that needs to be brought out into the light of reality. There's a relentless multi-billion dollar marketing machine that now sells kids and their parents everything from junk food and violent video games to bogus educational products and the family car. Drawing on the insights of health care professionals, children's advocates, and industry insiders, researchers are looking into the explosive growth of child marketing in the wake of deregulation, showing how youth marketers have used the latest advances in psychology, anthropology, and neuroscience to transform American children into one of the most powerful and profitable consumer demographics in the world. We should be pushing back against the wholesale commercialization of childhood and questioning the ethics of children's marketing and its impact on the health and well being of kids.

One commercial for a violent movie, a few sexual innuendos to get them to buy jeans, and a couple of ads urging them to eat junk food are not going to harm kids. But today, as never before, the lives of children are saturated with commercial marketing.

A generation ago, parents concerned about commercialism worried mainly about television. Today, children are also targeted through DVDs, video games, the Internet, MP3 players, and cell phones. In a world of marketing without borders, brand licensing and product placement prevail, marketing in schools escalates, babies are targeted, and friendships are exploited as companies increasingly rely on children to do their marketing for them.

Advertising sells children on more than products and brands. It also promotes values and behaviors. Childhood obesity, eating disorders, youth violence, sexualization, the erosion of children's creative play, materialistic values, and family stress are all linked to the commercialization of childhood.

By reaching out and indoctrinating the young, immature and gullible...the industry is, by extension, using children to influence their parent's buying preferences. The young are actually used as agents for the advertising industry. But it always goes back to the fact that "the free will of choice" is available to the responsible individuals.

As a society we hold parents responsible for the health, safety and well being of their children. Yet we have not held corporations accountable for spending billions of dollars on advertising that undermines their efforts. That is changing, there is a growing movement to reclaim childhood from corporate marketers.

The important lesson here is that we can now better understand the demise of those long ago, common sense, old school values that provided guidance for those of us from yesteryears. They (along with parenting in many cases) have quietly, over time, become victims of planned obsolescence. Today's progressive world has no interest in bygone days. They are the future...and the past is but history.

The key thing to remember is that human desires know no bounds...we are never satiated. If we replace an expensive disposable product with a permanent one, that just frees up income to spend on other extravagancies.

While our world is large enough to support all its inhabitants, it's not big enough to survive the greed of its individuals.

Chapter 7

While bullying has been around since the beginning of time, it has been developed and refined to a level never before imagined. From my perspective, growing up in rural America in the 40s and 50s, it was more of a one-on-one thing; but it has become the most powerful, manipulative tool known to the "civilized" world today. Starting at the top...from the president on down to individuals and organized groups, all using sarcasm and ridicule to mask the bullying. And if that doesn't work, you can just count on them moving into their shout-down mode.

We deal with it everyday in many different forms, some are just more blatant and commonplace. The freeways and surface streets are loaded with bullies riding your rear bumper because you're driving the speed limit... cutting in between you and the car ahead, the one you're trying to keep a safe distance from; and don't forget the one that sits on his horn because you're stopping for the yellow light before it turns red...as he picks up speed to go on through. The shout-down mode will often manifest itself in these situations also.

Race hustling, another form of bullying, has become a

"cottage industry" in the United States. Groups such as "Hispanic Voice" obtain their power by intimidating anyone with dissenting views. If anyone disagrees with them or dares to think for themselves, they are ostracized by the community as a race traitor.

This is classic socialist-Marxist silencing of opposing views through politically correct intimidation (bullying), the incessant impugning of one's character, motives and beliefs. The individual is marginalized to keep the masses in line. It's a social, racial and gender grievance strategy that has long since been mastered by the NAACP, La Raza, NOW and other like-minded Marxist-based organizations.

Of course we've all been reading and hearing about youngsters all around the country taking their own lives because of peer bullying. Today's younger people are committing suicide (for various reasons) at rates unheard of in my time.

Back in the 1920s, the intelligentsias on both sides of the Atlantic were loudly protesting the execution of political radicals Sacco and Vanzetti, after what they claimed was an unfair trial. Supreme Court Justice Oliver Wendell Holmes wrote to his young leftist friend Harold Laski, pointing out that there were "a thousand-fold worse cases" involving black defendants, "but the world does not worry over them."

Holmes said, "I cannot but ask myself why so much greater interest in red than black."

To put it bluntly, it was a question of whose cow was gored. That is, what groups were in vogue at the moment among the intelligentsia? Blacks clearly were not.

The current media and political crusade against "bullying"

in schools seems likewise to be based on what groups are in vogue at the moment. For years, there have been local newspaper stories about black kids in schools in New York and Philadelphia beating up Asian classmates, some beaten so badly as to require medical treatment.

The national media hears no evil, sees no evil and speaks no evil. Asian Americans are not in vogue today, just as blacks were not in vogue in the 1920s.

Meanwhile, the media focuses on bullying directed against youngsters who are homosexual. Gays are in vogue now. Most of the stories about the bullying of gays in schools are about words directed against them, not about their suffering the violence that has long been directed against Asian youngsters or about the failure of the authorities to do anything serious to stop black kids from beating up Asian kids.

Where youngsters are victims of violence, whether for being gay, Asian or whatever, that is where the authorities need to step in. No decent person wants to see kids harassed, by words or deeds.

There is still a difference between words and deeds... and it is a difference we do not need to let ourselves be stampeded into ignoring. The First Amendment to the Constitution of the United States guarantees freedom of speech, and like any other freedom...it can be abused.

If we are going to take away every constitutional right that has been abused by somebody, we are going to end up with no constitutional rights. Already, on too many college campuses, there are vaguely worded speech codes that can punish students for words that may hurt someone's feelings...but only of those groups that are in vogue.

Women can say anything they want to men, or blacks to whites, with impunity. But strong words in the other direction can bring down the wrath of the campus thought-police, as well as punishment that can include suspension or expulsion of students.

Is this what we want in our public schools?

The school authorities can ignore the beating of Asian kids but homosexual organizations have enough political clout that they cannot be ignored. Moreover, there are enough avowed homosexuals among journalists that they have their own National Lesbian and Gay Journalists Association...so continuing media publicity will ensure that the authorities will have to "do something."

Political pressures to "do something" have been behind many counterproductive and even dangerous policies.

A grand jury report about bullying in the schools of San Mateo County in California brought all sorts of expressions of concern from school authorities...but no definition of "bullying" or any specifics about just what they plan to do about it. Meanwhile, a law has been passed in California that mandates teaching in public schools about the achievements of gays. Whether this will do anything to stop either verbal or physical abuse of gay kids is very doubtful.

It will advance the agenda of homosexual organizations and can turn homosexuality into yet another subject of which only certain words are permitted on one side. Our schools are already too lacking in the basics of education to squander even more time on propaganda for politically correct causes that are in vogue. We do not need to create special privileges in the name of equal rights.

And no individual, group or organization is too big to be bullied.

I just read where a liberal group apparently has succeeded in its efforts to have conservative commentator Pat Buchanan dropped from MSNBC shows. Color of Change announced that the cable network has confirmed that Buchanan has been suspended indefinitely.

The group had been pushing for Buchanan's dismissal since October. An email alert the group sent Tuesday proclaimed: "Pat Buchanan and his white supremacist ideology will no longer be on TV." The email went on to say that MSNBC President Phil Griffin confirmed to the group that Buchanan was "suspended indefinitely." However, the group stated that it hopes the suspension will be made permanent.

Executive Director Rashad Robinson said in a statement, "ColorOfChange.org welcomes MSNBC's decision to indefinitely suspend Pat Buchanan. However, it's time for MSNBC to permanently end their relationship with Pat Buchanan and the hateful, outdated ideology he represents. We appreciate this first step and urge MSNBC to take the important final step to ensure that their brand is no longer associated with Buchanan's history of passing off white supremacy ideology as mainstream political commentary."

Update: Several weeks later MSNBC did in fact, kowtow to the Color of Change organization and permanently dismissed Pat Buchanan.

Color of Change has launched a number of campaigns against other conservatives, including advertising boycotts against Glenn Beck.

Another example: ABC's entertainment chief says he just

doesn't understand complaints made by a transgender group about the network's new sitcom.

The comedy series, "Work It," debuted last week portraying two men who dress as women to land jobs in a tough economy. The Nielsen Company reported that 6.2 million people watched the first episode. The Gay & Lesbian Alliance Against Defamation said it was offensive to the transgender community because it made fun of the idea of men wearing women's clothing.

Interesting how time and progressivism has changed perspectives...I immediately flashed back to Dustin Hoffman as Tootsie in 1982...30 years ago. It was funny and no one came forward to condemn the comedy... because that's all it was, comedy!

Actress Cynthia Nixon (Walter E. Nixon, a Texas-born radio journalist's daughter) recently found herself at the center of controversy when The New York Times quoted her as saying that she was "gay by choice." She further stated, "I understand that for many people it's not, but for me it's a choice, and you don't get to define my 'gayness' for me." Nixon also told the Times, "A certain section of our community is very concerned that it not be seen as a choice, because if it's a choice, then we could opt out. I say it doesn't matter if we flew here or we swam here."

Best known for playing Miranda Hobbes on "Sex and the City," Nixon is engaged to a woman who she's been involved with for eight years. Before that she spent 15 years with a man who fathered her two children.

Gay rights activists were angered by Nixon's remarks. Among them was Truth Wins Out founder Wayne Besen, whose organization monitors programs that claim to cure people of same-sex attractions. He says Nixon's comments could be used to force people into such programs.

Once again, marginalize the individual to keep the masses in line. The difference? Bullying and the Gay & Lesbian community are in vogue today.

Bullying is especially affective when directed at those demeaned as being out of touch with reality in our new progressive world. Today's Christians are being ridiculed and marginalized by non-believers, like never before.

When millions of Muslims danced in the streets, praising Allah for the "blessings" brought about by Mohamed Atta and his Band of Brothers on 9/11, we were counseled to be tolerant and respectful of those celebrants' religious views.

However, when a young quarterback, said by all experts to be grossly lacking in skill and technique...repeatedly does the improbable, he is ridiculed for his faith in God. When Tebow, Denver Broncos' quarterback, praises God (by kneeling on one knee) for such blessings, he is summarily vilified and mocked. If he was to launch into an end-zone victory dance, replete with taunting of the opponent and chest-pounding, he'd be lauded for his "passionate self-expression and unabashed appreciation of so momentous an accomplishment."

Give me Tebow and many more like him...any day. Modesty, class and cognizance of context are in woefully short supply today...as is common sense.

Last week the "Backyard Skeptics" (a group of atheists who, for whatever reason, feel a need to discredit Christianity by placing negative billboards along our freeways) continued its ongoing argument built around the classic disagreement of science versus religion (but of course Islam is never challenged). The problem is that neither theist nor atheist seems to understand what science is. There is a vast difference between what "scientists believe" and what "science predicts." Most renowned scientists of the past held strong religious convictions.

Their convictions had nothing to do with scientific theories or experiments. Science has nothing to say about creation, or what anything really is. Newton had no idea why gravity existed or where it came from, but assuming gravity existed he was able to explain how it affected our world and the universe.

Science does not ask the question, "Who or what created the electron or the proton or the neutrino or life." Science is the continuous process of postulating and testing theories that predict how something reacts given a set of physical circumstances. Any theory aimed at explaining the "creation" of man or why elementary particles exist, is not science, it is metaphysics. Scientific theories hypothesize the occurrence of the "big bang" as a starting point for the beginning of our universe.

The basic elements of physics, time, space, force, energy, etc. cannot be extended to the time before the big bang... so science has nothing to say about how or why the big bang occurred. While it is correct to say that science is never settled, it is also true that legitimate science has nothing to say about the creation of man or life before the "big bang."

Karl Marx once said, "Religion is the opiate of the masses."

That may well have been the case in his day, but today who isn't on Facebook, Twitter, Yahoo or Google on a regular basis via their cell, iPad, laptop or home computer?

The Internet is the new opiate of the masses.

Interestingly enough though, the fact is that most of the bullying against Christians (and other groups) is facilitated through the Internet.

The progressivism that's inundating every aspect of our lives is the main reason we're on this very slippery slope today.

I have often wondered why Conservatives are called the "right" and Liberals are called the "left." Well, by chance I stumbled upon the origin...and the answer:

> "The heart of the wise inclines to the right,
> but the heart of the fool to the left."

> Ecclesiastes 10:2 (NIV)

Can't get any clearer than that.

> "Error of Opinion may be tolerated where Reason is left free to combat it."

> Thomas Jefferson

CHAPTER 8

While Christianity has been on both sides of global bullying tactics since the beginning of religion, the bullying and ridicule "crusade" against Christians is unprecedented in America today. But what makes it even more disturbing to me is that it seems to be in line with our ever-growing Muslim population. We already know (those of us who value the lessons of history) that historically speaking, these two religions don't make for a homogeneous neighborhood. And even if history is just history to you, look around at your current, ever-changing world. If the conflict between the two religions is not physically deadly (as in many countries), it is being fought in the courts of the countries they have adopted as their own.

The bullying of America's Christians is still in its infancy compared to the history of global contempt for the Jewish people.

The dirty little secret of America's higher education:

On campuses across the country pro-terror groups stage political demonstrations that have the tone and content of Hitler's Nuremberg rallies every single day.

Anti-Semitism and anti-Israel hatred are not only tolerated in our universities, they are in vogue. The atmosphere on campus today recalls that of Germany in the 1930s when Hitler was laying the groundwork for the Holocaust. Muslim students are allowed to intimidate Jewish students. They are allowed to bring "Islamist" preachers of hate onto campuses with unapologetically vile messages that would cause the KKK to blush.

Like yesterday's "good Germans," members of the academic community look the other way because of political correctness. Muslims are an "oppressed minority group"...and no one dares oppose their agenda.

Muslim hate groups, on campuses, spotlight the radical Muslim Students Association, a group created years ago by the Muslim Brotherhood as part of a subversive network of organizations dedicated to the overthrow of America's society. This supposedly "benign" cultural, campus organization has actually been the breeding ground for some of today's international terrorist leadership.

This week on "The Hal Lindsey Report" (February 10th, 2012):

In September of 2011, members of the Canadian government put their signatures to a document called "The Ottawa Protocol to Combat Anti-Semitism." At the signing ceremony, a member of the Canadian parliament, Professor Irwin Cotler remarked, "Anti-Semitism is not only the longest known form of hatred in the history of humanity, it is the only form of hatred that is truly global."

Prime Minister Stephen Harper noted, "Those who would hate and destroy the Jewish people would ultimately hate and destroy the rest of us as well."

Prime Minister Harper's implication is clear. Those who would destroy the Jews, then destroy the rest of us as well, are evil. Or, at least, driven by evil. That's why God Himself deemed it necessary to publicly promise to curse those who curse or harm His chosen people. Conversely, He also publicly promised to bless those who bless or protect and benefit the Jews.

Now, before you dismiss these words as the ravings of a lunatic "Christian Zionist," let me remind you of something you may have overlooked or forgotten. Maybe you've never even heard this. After the believing Church has been "raptured" from this earth and the time of great Tribulation has fallen upon the world, Jesus Christ will return to the earth in His promised Second Coming. After saving the Jews and the world from utter destruction, He will then sit in judgment.

Did you know that the criteria He will use to judge those Gentiles who stand before Him (the Jews will be judged separately) will be how they treated His people during the time of Tribulation? Matthew 25 describes what will happen.

And you thought the cry of "anti-Semitism" was like the young shepherd boy crying, "Wolf." Not so, Anti-Semitism then and now is very important to God.

We are witnessing an explosion of anti-Semitic incidents across the world, from the Muslim enclaves of Europe to the "Occupy Wall Street" demonstrations here in America. Even the current administration displays a disturbing attitude of anti-Semitism...practiced by prominent officials even if not openly espoused. And Bible prophecy tells us that it will only increase as we approach the end of this Age.

Folks, if this tells us one thing for certain, it's this:

How we treat the Jews and the Jewish nation is serious business.

> "For evil to flourish, all that is needed is for good people to do nothing."
>
> Edmund Burke

CHAPTER 9

"Congress shall make no law respecting an establishment of religion, or prohibiting the free exercise thereof..."

Amendment I, United States Constitution

Freedom of religion is a Constitutional right. Indeed, it is our nation's most foundational right.

In contrast, the convenience of government-mandated free contraceptives from religious institutions in violation of their fundamental theology is not.

Those two basic truths settle the merits of this week's sudden collision between the Obama Administration and religious institutions.

Importantly, this is not a debate about contraceptives themselves. Whether one condones or opposes contraceptive use is wholly irrelevant. Birth control has been legal and beyond prohibition since Griswold v. Connecticut in 1965, and that's not about to change. Furthermore, if the Obama Administration favors universal contraceptive dispensation, nothing prevents it from asking voters to add that to the federal government's existing list of expenditures. But it is not entitled to compel free religious charities to do so in violation of the First Amendment.

After all, America's very existence stems from European refugees who were so desperate for freedom from government interference with their religious practice that they opted to abandon beloved friends and family, leave their homes, journey across a treacherous ocean, confront an unfamiliar and hostile new continent and endure deprivation, starvation and attacks to achieve it. Ultimately, our Founding Fathers considered religious freedom so fundamental to a just society that they placed it first among the specific individual protections amended to the Constitution.

Today, however, the fact that some liberals demand "equilibrium" between that basic First Amendment right and the Obama Administration's contraceptive policy preferences, illustrates the gravity of our current Constitutional crisis. If this administration behaves this crudely and thuggishly during an election year, what might await the nation in a second term?

All of this, of course, is a natural consequence of ObamaCare. And it recalls once again Nancy Pelosi's infamous admonition that, *"We have to pass the bill so that you can find out what's in it."*

And have we ever...

Last month, Obama's Health and Human Services Department (HHS) finally got around to determining that "what's in" ObamaCare is a requirement that employers provide contraceptives for free. Consequently, religious institutions such as hospitals, homeless shelters, schools and charities would be forced to follow partisan reproductive policy over fundamental theological principle.

As a result, thousands of private charitable organizations would be prohibited from the free exercise of religion. On the one hand, after all, such institutions' theology requires charity. On the other hand, their theology compels respect for what they in good faith consider human life.

Under our Constitution, the federal government is not entitled to demand that dilemma.

Ironically, as HHS issued its mandate last month, the United States Supreme Court unanimously rejected Obama Administration overreach into religious freedom. In Hosanna-Tabor Evangelical Lutheran Church v. Equal Employment Opportunity Commission, the Court reaffirmed the right of religious institutions to make ministerial employment decisions without federal micromanagement.

Public opinion, fortunately, already appears to side with the First Amendment over this new ObamaCare intrusion. Despite the fact that the American electorate favors private access to contraceptive options as a general proposition, Rasmussen (a polling organization) reports that voters reject the Obama Administration's mandate by a 50 percent to 39 percent margin.

As for those "conservative" House Democrats who cast pivotal votes in favor of ObamaCare in the spring of 2010 based on Obama's promise of theological protections, former Congresswoman Kathy Dahlkemper (D-Pennsylvania) explicitly stated that she wouldn't have voted for the bill knowing what we now know:

"I would have never voted for the final version of the bill

if I expected the Obama Administration to force Catholic hospitals and Catholic colleges and universities to pay for contraception. We worked hard to prevent abortion funding in health care and to include clear conscience protections for those with moral objections to abortion and contraceptive devices."

Too bad she voted to pass the bill before finding out "what's in it," as former Speaker Pelosi said. That largely explains why today she is a "former" Congresswoman and Pelosi is a "former" Speaker.

Odds are, that the Obama Administration's awakening to the unexpected backlash resulting from its deliberate disregard for religious freedom, will be backtracking and acting as if its reversal illustrates its "moderation" and "willingness to compromise." Any such reversal, however, would stand hollow given the knowledge that a second term would allow "him" to reverse course and once again...impose the contraceptive mandate, with electoral impunity. As hollow in fact, as his original false pledge that fundamental religious freedom would be safe from ObamaCare.

Again, the issue isn't whether contraceptives are moral or immoral, good public policy or bad public policy. The issue is whether we will preserve our nation's most basic freedom of conscience against an Obama Administration so hostile toward America's fundamental principles that it would sacrifice them at its new altar of ideological purity.

The United States' Roman Catholic Bishops made a Faustian bargain with the Obama administration when they backed the mandated insurance coverage plan. Now, for all their support, the Obama administration has played them like a Stradivarius.

To frame this issue as a Roman Catholic opposition to birth control vs. the federal government's ruling that all insurance plans must cover reproductive health issues is superficial.

First, many religious groups besides the Catholic Church oppose some or all contraceptive/abortion matters. The Catholic Church is just the largest target. The real issue, in my opinion, is the administration's cynical attitude toward religious organizations as a whole, which boils down to a First Amendment issue: The right of religious organizations to proclaim and practice their religious beliefs without interference from the government.

Notice how the Obama administration has nuanced the First Amendment's freedom of religion to "freedom of worship." President Obama once made reference to *"those bitter people who cling to their religion and guns." Could he have been referring to the First and Second Amendments?*

The political furor over President Obama's birth-control mandate continues to grow, even among those for whom contraception poses no moral qualms, and one needn't be a theologian to understand why. Our country is being exposed to the raw political control that is the core of the Obama health-care plan, and Americans are seeing clearly for the first time how this will violate pluralism and liberty.

Obama has now given us a "compromise" so religious organizations don't have to pay for abortions. Abortions and contraception have to be paid for by insurance companies. So who pays for the insurance? We all do, including those of us who have a religious aversion to abortion.

Insurance companies will collect from the government

(our taxes), not the religious organizations. This is not a compromise; it's a bait-and-switch. Insurance premiums will go up, and insurance companies will be attacked for raising rates.

Religious liberty won't be protected from the entitlement mentality until ObamaCare is repealed.

The coming Supreme Court decision about the constitutionality of the Affordable Care Act's individual mandate will have profound implications for government control over the doctor-patient relationship. Simply put, if the federal government can mandate that all Americans must have health insurance, it is only a short step to strict government mandates about how doctors must practice medicine.

Under ObamaCare, medical care will transition from what is appropriate for the individual patient to what is appropriate from government's perspective. Furthermore, the cost of care will be a significant factor, *with government, not doctors and/or patients, ultimately deciding if a treatment is worthwhile.*

The groundwork for tighter government control over medical decisions was laid in Obama's 2009 stimulus legislation, which charged the Institute of Medicine with determining what topics the government should study in its "comparative effectiveness research."

Most of the institute's 100 priorities relate to Medicare. The top three call for comparing the value of medication vs. surgery; treating hearing loss by teaching sign language rather than relying on cochlear implants, and clinical treatments vs. recommending exercise.

The institute also included many priority topics in cancer treatment, such as "watchful waiting" compared to actual medical treatment for localized prostate cancer. The institute's report lists many other research targets involving the "relative" value of drugs, diagnostics, medical treatments and other interventions.

While comparative effectiveness research can be a valuable tool in helping doctors make good decisions, it also can be a dangerous tool in which government, not doctors, controls the medical care we receive. Since the government pays for an ever-growing share of medical care, it inevitably will place a high priority on finding the lowest-cost treatment.

The administration has already demonized physicians as largely responsible for the high costs of health care in America. Obama, for example, has claimed that surgeons are more likely to do amputations for diabetics because they get paid more for these procedures than for prescribing medication.

There are other ways the law threatens the quality of patient care. To finance the health overhaul law, Medicare payments will be cut by $500 billion at the same time the bulk of baby boomers will be hitting retirement age.

In addition to these cuts, ObamaCare created a new Independent Payment Advisory Board with powers to further limit the growth of Medicare spending. Fifteen un-elected technocrats will have the authority to cut Medicare spending to stay within set spending targets. Their decisions are not subject to judicial review, and it will be difficult for Congress to overrule board decisions.

By September 1, 2013, the board must submit its first draft proposals to limit Medicare spending. The secretary of Health and Human Services must act the next year to implement the proposals unless Congress passes an alternative plan that achieves the required Medicare savings. If Congress fails, the original board proposal to cut Medicare will take effect. Thus, the board, armed with government data, will have the power to limit Medicare spending and thereby ration medical care.

We already see this happening in the programs government controls now. Drugs are already rationed under Medicaid...for example, with many patients facing restricted access to the newest and best drugs. Rationing of care already exists under Medicare with...for example, its lifetime limit of 100 days for care in a skilled nursing facility and restrictions on the number of days allowed for a hospital stay.

The transformation of Medicare from an insurance system to a system directing the practice of medicine is defended as necessary to save the program and to standardize what is "appropriate" care for Medicare patients. This creates a significant conflict of interest when the government is the payer and also determines what constitutes appropriate care.

The autonomy of patients and clinical judgment of physicians will unquestionably be undermined by ObamaCare.

For continued progress in medical innovation and to achieve the personalized care that 21st century medicine will bring, it is vital to move away from centralized government dominance of the health sector and toward a new system that rewards payers and providers for providing quality medical care. That means putting patients, not government, first.

None of this should come as a surprise. The ObamaCare bill contained 700 references to the Secretary "shall," another 200 to the Secretary "may," and 139 to the Secretary "determines." So the Secretary of Health may and shall determine pretty much anything she wants, as the rubes amongst the Catholic hierarchy are belatedly discovering.

The bigger the Big Government, the smaller everything else: The pillars of our civil society are slowly...but relentlessly, being removed from the public arena and relegated to the ever-growing phenomenon of *obsolescence*. Even the individual...as my generation remembers him, is disappearing into the system...progressive collectivism. Our government and many others believe in a one-size-fits all national government...uniformity, conformity, for all except favored cronies. It is a doomed experiment... and on the morning after, it will take a lot more than a morning-after pill to make it all go away.

Obama is treating our constitutional First Amendment rights as revocable privileges from our government, not as inalienable rights from our creator.

Anyone who thinks the attacks on the Roman Catholic Church...and Christians in general, are about contraception is wrong. It's about religious freedom and devaluing faith.

Ask your Jewish friends what can happen when a state demonizes a people or a faith. Is this merely the beginning? Just asking...

> "The more energetic the political activity in the country, the greater is the loss to spiritual life."
> Aleksandr Solzhenitsyn

CHAPTER 10

Margaret Higgins Sanger (September 14, 1879 - September 6, 1966) was an American sex educator, nurse, and birth control activist. Sanger coined the term birth control, opened the first birth control clinic in the United States, and established Planned Parenthood. Sanger's efforts contributed to the landmark United States Supreme Court case that legalized contraception in the United States. Sanger is a frequent target of criticism by opponents of the legalization of abortion, based primarily upon her racial views and support of eugenics, but she remains an iconic figure for the American reproductive rights movement.

In 1914, Sanger launched The Woman Rebel, an eight-page monthly newsletter that promoted contraception using the slogan "No Gods, No Masters." Sanger, collaborating with anarchist friends, coined the term birth control as a more candid alternative to euphemisms such as family limitation and proclaimed that each woman should be "the absolute mistress of her own body." In those early years of Sanger's activism, she viewed birth control as a free speech issue, and when she started publishing The Woman Rebel, one of her goals was to provoke a legal challenge to the federal anti-obscenity laws which banned dissemination of information about contraception.

After WW I, Sanger shifted away from radical politics, and founded the American Birth Control League (ABCL) in 1921 to enlarge her base of supporters to include the middle class. The founding principles of the ABCL were as follows:

We hold that children should be (1st) Conceived in love, (2nd) Born of the mother's conscious desire, (3) Only begotten under conditions which render possible the heritage of health. Therefore we hold that every woman must possess the power and freedom to prevent conception except when these conditions can be satisfied.

In 1929, Sanger formed the National Committee on Federal Legislation for Birth Control in order to lobby for legislation to overturn restrictions on contraception. That effort failed to achieve success, so Sanger ordered a diaphragm from Japan in 1932, in order to provoke a decisive battle in the courts. The diaphragm was confiscated by the United States government, and Sanger's subsequent legal challenge led to a 1936 court decision which overturned an important provision of the Comstock laws which prohibited physicians from obtaining contraceptives. This court victory motivated the American Medical Association in 1937 to adopt contraception as a normal medical service and a key component of medical school curriculums.

As part of her efforts to promote birth control, Sanger found common cause with proponents of eugenics, believing that they both sought to "assist the race toward the elimination of the unfit." Sanger was a proponent of negative eugenics, which aims to improve human hereditary traits through social intervention by reducing reproduction by those considered unfit. Sanger's eugenic policies included an exclusionary immigration policy, free access to birth control methods and full family planning autonomy for the able-minded, and compulsory segregation or sterilization for the profoundly retarded. In her book The Pivot of Civilization, she advocated coercion to prevent the "undeniably feeble-minded" from procreating. Although Sanger supported negative eugenics, she asserted that eugenics alone was not sufficient, and that birth control was essential to achieve her goals.

In contrast with eugenicists who advocated euthanasia for the unfit, Sanger wrote, "we do not believe that the community could or should send to the lethal chamber the defective progeny resulting from irresponsible and unintelligent breeding." Similarly, Sanger denounced the aggressive and lethal Nazi eugenics program. In addition, Sanger believed the responsibility for birth control should remain in the hands of able-minded individual parents rather than the state, and that self-determining motherhood was the only unshakable foundation for racial betterment.

Complementing her eugenics policies, Sanger also supported restrictive immigration policies. In "A Plan for Peace," a 1932 essay, she proposed a congressional department to address population problems. She also recommended that immigration exclude those "whose condition is known to be detrimental to the stamina of the race," and that sterilization and segregation be applied to those with incurable, hereditary disabilities.

Sanger believed that lighter-skinned races were superior to darker-skinned races, but would not tolerate bigotry among her staff, nor any refusal to work within interracial projects. Her contemporaries in the African-American community supported her efforts.

The "Negro Project" was an effort to deliver birth control to poor African Americans. Sanger wanted the Negro Project to include black ministers in leadership roles, but other supervisors did not. To emphasize the benefits of involving black community leaders, she wrote, "We do not want the word to go out that we want to exterminate the Negro population and the minister is the man who can straighten out that idea if it ever occurs to any of their more rebellious members." Numerous Sanger detractors, including Angela Davis and the pro-life movement, have used this quote to support their claims that Sanger was racist. However, supporters counter that Sanger, in writing that letter, "recognized that elements within the black community might mistakenly associate the Negro Project with racist sterilization campaigns in the Jim Crow South, unless clergy and other community leaders spread the word that the Project had a humanitarian aim."

Sanger's family planning advocacy always focused on contraception, rather than abortion. It was not until the mid-1960s, after Sanger's death, that the reproductive rights movement expanded its scope to include abortion rights as well as contraception. Sanger was opposed to abortions, both because they were dangerous for the mother, and because she believed that life should not be terminated after conception. In her book Woman and the New Race, she wrote, "While there are cases where even the law recognizes an abortion as justifiable if recommended by a physician, I assert that the hundreds of thousands of abortions performed in America each year are a disgrace to civilization."

Historian Rodger Streitmatter concluded that Sanger's opposition to abortion stemmed from concerns for the dangers to the mother, rather than moral concerns. However, in her 1938 autobiography, Sanger noted that her opposition to abortion was based on the taking of life: "In 1916 we explained what contraception was; that abortion was the wrong way, no matter how early it was performed...it was taking a life; that contraception was the better way, the safer way. It took a little time, a little trouble, but was well worth while in the long run, because life had not yet begun." And in her book Family Limitation, Sanger wrote, "No one can doubt that there are times when an abortion is justifiable, but they will become unnecessary when care is taken to prevent conception. This is the only cure for abortions."

We have a mixed bag here with arguable pros and cons that will never be settled...but for me, birth control is a "personal responsibility." The individual should be "accountable" for his/her actions and the consequences therein. Whether by contraceptives or abstinence, responsibility is the sole burden of the participants. Abortion should not be an option unless the mother's life/health is at risk.

> "A government big enough to give you everything you want, is strong enough to take everything you have."
>
> Gerald R. Ford

CHAPTER 11

I'm going to wade into some deep water here, but it's not something I haven't expounded on before. Our progressive government's education curriculum aside... the progressive liberals, their compliant liberal media and even many in the intelligentsias community continue to deny that cultural factors appear to influence the learning curve of an array of ethnicities. And when you add the "uncaring students from uncaring families" the overall differential becomes conspicuous.

Below is an article from the Associated Press written by "our" mainstream media:

Good teachers are the key to accelerating academic achievement by Hispanic and black students to levels on par with their white and Asian counterparts, but poor and minority children are consistently assigned the worst instructors, according to a study released today.

"We know that great teachers have the power to help students catch up when they're behind," said Arun Ramanathan, executive director of The Education Trust-West, which carried out the 18-month-long study. "But you can't catch up when you don't have access to the best teachers."

The study tracked 1 million students and 17,000 teachers over three years.

It is part of a growing body of research adding weight to the case for better evaluation methods of teachers, including an end to seniority-based layoffs in favor of performance-based measures and more stringent tenure standards.

Teachers unions have largely and strongly opposed such changes. And yes, the unions are contributors to the educational quagmire of progressivism, indifference and ineptness.

Although the Education Trust study only analyzed the Los Angeles Unified School District...the nation's second largest with 665,000 students, its findings hold true elsewhere; the same thing is happening across the country...according to co-authors Orville Jackson and Carrie Hahnel.

The study analyzed teachers and student's scores from standardized state tests, coming up with effectiveness rankings for the teachers. Researchers acknowledged that test scores are not the only measure of teaching quality. It analyzed where more effective teachers were located, how many were laid off in 2009, and how students fared under effective teachers.

Results showed that the more effective teachers were concentrated in schools in more affluent areas and that highly effective teachers were more likely to leave low-performing schools.

The liberal, politically correct spin on the above article is a crock.

And the researchers' suggested solution...?

The study recommended policy changes to help improve access to quality teachers, including better professional development of teachers and evaluation methods, incentives to retain top teachers in high-poverty schools, reform state laws mandating seniority-based layoffs and oversight to ensure that top teachers are spread equitably among schools. Another crock!

What one needs to understand is that these studies are almost always implemented and funded by the government, the same entity that rejects any correlation to cultural background or even the lack of importance some families place on education.

I am a high school dropout myself and I attribute that shortcoming to the fact that...even though I attended school through the 10th grade, the value of education was never a subject of conversation in my family.

Getting back to the study...I guess it would seem, from the liberals' perspective, that somehow the system is systematically rounding up all its highly effective teachers and re-assigning them to the higher performing schools in the more prosperous areas. The worst...or leftover teachers are then assigned to the ranks of the under-performing schools in the low-rent, poverty districts. Well, at least that way everything matches up.

Of course, some of the highly effective teachers will leave the performance challenged schools for different reasons. I recognize the fact that some will leave due to the frustrating futility of fighting a prevailing backdrop of indifference. Others may find the low performing school's poverty area atmosphere less than comfortable as a workplace...or even un-accepting of outsiders.

All the above begs the eternal question...which came first, the chicken or the egg?

My question is less ambiguous...from my point of view of course. Which came first, the high performing schools or highly effective teachers? The low performing schools or unmotivated students?

The chicken or the egg causality dilemma is commonly stated as "which came first, the chicken or the egg?" To ancient philosophers, the question about the first chicken or egg also evoked the questions of how life and the universe in general began. I'm suggesting we could apply that same basic principle to our educational organizations.

Cultural references to the chicken and egg tend to point out the futility of identifying the first case of a circular cause and consequence. It could be considered that in this approach lies the most fundamental nature of the question. An unembellished answer is somewhat obvious, as egg-laying species pre-date the existence of chickens. However, the metaphorical view sets a metaphysical argument to the dilemma. To better understand its metaphorical meaning, the question could be reformulated as: "Which came first, X (high-performing schools) that can't come without Y (motivated students), or Y (low-performing school) that can't come without X (un-motivated/apathetic students)?"

And yes, of course...there are teachers that should be weeded out...but don't tell me the problem is that the "system" systematically and routinely manipulates the placement of teachers to benefit the more prosperous areas.

Our laws and government policies reflect an assumption that if any significant statistical difference between racial or ethnic groups in employment, income or educational achievements can only be the result of them being treated differently by others.

The government has sued businesses when the representation of different groups among their employees differed substantially from their proportion at large. But, no matter how the human race is broken down into its components, whether by race, sex, geographic region or whatever...glaring disparities in achievements have been the rule...not the exception.

Anyone who watches professional basketball games knows that the star players are by no means a representative example of our population as a whole.

Most professional golfers who participate in PGA tournaments have never won a single tournament, but Arnold Palmer, Jack Nicklaus and Tiger Woods have each won dozens of tournaments.

These and numerous other disparities are resolutely ignored by those shrill voices that routinely denounce disparities as suspicious at best and even sinister...worse case. Of course, certain disparities just don't support their agenda, and that is to generate more and more government handouts and assistance for the under-achievers.

Higher achieving groups, whether classes, races or whatever...are often blamed for the failure of other groups to achieve. Politicians and intellectuals, especially, tend to conceive of social questions in terms that allow them to take on the role of being on the side of the angels against the forces of evil.

This can be a huge disservice to those individuals and groups who are lagging behind, for it leads them to focus on a sense of grievance and victim-hood, rather than on how they can lift themselves up instead of trying to pull other people down to their level.

Unfortunately, this is a worldwide phenomenon...and a sad commentary on the down side of mankind, or in the bigger picture...*"world brotherhood."*

By 1905 two African American leaders dominated the debate over the best course for racial advancement in America. Booker T. Washington became the best-known spokesman following the death of Frederick Douglass in 1895.

Foremost among those who rose to challenge Washington was William Edward Burghardt Du Bois, who had a different plan. The two men became archrivals. Washington even hired spies to keep an eye on Du Bois.

Booker T. Washington did not think that social equality of the races was as important as economic equality. He said:

> *"The wisest among my race understand that the agitation of questions of social equality is the extremist folly, and that progress in the enjoyment of all the privileges that will come to us...must be the result of severe and constant struggle rather than of artificial forcing."*

Washington, Atlanta Exposition Address, 1895.

At the time, Du Bois wrote to Washington and said of the Atlanta Address:

"My Dear Mr. Washington: Let me heartily congratulate you upon your phenomenal success in Atlanta...it was a word fitly spoken."

Du Bois later called Washington's Atlanta Exposition Address the "Atlanta Compromise," because it compromised social equality of the races in order to gain economic equality.

Since the beginning, the one constant element in life is that we learn as we go...but the problem is that life's learning curve allows for a vast array of variables. And one of life's unspoken truths is that we, as individuals, must prove (and reprove) ourselves everyday of our lives. Many are unwilling, unmotivated and/or just too lazy to go the extra mile required for that daily demonstration of ones principles and character. Self-respect and personal pride are often rationalized away and left along the wayside as their journey begins to ask more and more of them. As they fall further and further behind, the "it's not my fault" mentality works to compromise any lingering self-esteem...even as they're reaching for the entitlement crutch.

The desire of one man to live on the fruits of another's labor is the original sin of the world.

CHAPTER 12

I recently read an article exposing more of the obscene compensation for administrators in California's UC system where administrators almost outnumber teachers. They live in the same dream world as the Occupy rabble they "educated." And there lies the problem. Except for a small number of super-wealthy college students who don't plan on working after graduation anyway, the rest "should" expect to get a job in the "real world" so they can pay off the loans that pay the salaries of their teachers and administrators. The educational system that stole their money may owe them a living, but the rest of us don't.

In that article, an assistant professor (name unimportant... in the bigger picture) was quoted when he asked this rhetorical question, "What kind of future are we creating for our students if we saddle them with debt they can't pay?" My first thought was, what a hypocrite... you're certainly not offering to accept any less for your service.

But what really struck me was the article's picture of this individual sitting at his desk (Cal State Fullerton)...and on the wall, above his desk was a large framed picture of

"Karl Marx." Blatant socialism in our education system... and don't ever doubt that it has permeated the system top to bottom.

But back to the "bigger picture question," "What kind of future are we creating for our students if Karl Marx is being promoted as a way of life by their instructors?"

The problem for the Occupy students is that there is no warning label on courses like (and these are real): "The Science of Superheroes" at UC Irvine, "Arguing with Judge Judy" and "Popular 'Logic' on TV Judge Shows" at UC Berkeley...and degrees such as "Queer Musicology" at UCLA. The labels should say, "Caution, this course will not prepare you to work in the real world, get a job or support yourself."

There are simple solutions to our un-funded liabilities and out-of-control retirement benefits in the UC system. Enroll UC and government employees (teachers, police, fire included) in Social Security as their only state-sponsored retirement. Benefits not to start until they reach 65.

Tenure, which doesn't exist in the real world, is gone. They will occasionally get unpaid sabbaticals to look for a real job to prove that no one will pay them one-fourth of what they now earn. Their pay, retirement and benefits must be posted on their office door so that their students realize their administrators and/or teachers are the 1 percent.

UC employees can no longer compare salaries and/or benefits with other teaching institutions. That is a merry-go-round of increases based on nothing in the real world. If they want a raise they can look for a private-sector job or transfer to another institution.

Finally, no government employee, politician or teacher can send his or her children to private schools until we have a voucher system. The system would self-correct just as ObamaCare would be repealed if politicians were enrolled like the rest of us.

Continually rising college tuition costs have been made possible by ever increasing government-backed student loans. This is similar to the housing mess where increasing home prices were fueled by unbridled lending practices also backed by the government. Universities now have little incentive to manage their personnel and administrative costs because they can just pass them along in the form of higher tuition, that their customers (students) will just borrow from enabling government-backed lenders. Hopefully, students will finally figure this out and redirect their scorn from the taxpayers to the administrators and politicians who have built this house of cards.

History instruction in public schools, especially at the elementary level, is in poor shape. Survey after survey shows that most Americans really, "Don't know much about history." We hear a lot about the need to improve reading, math and science scores, but not much emphasis is given to the quality of history instruction, despite the likelihood that historically aware voters ought to have a better understanding of the issues. This is, in part, because there is only so much time each day to schedule all that is currently required to be taught. Since history scores are not used to determine which schools are considered failing under either the "No Child Left Behind" or "Race to the Top" programs, time for social studies instruction has been reduced.

Along with the decrease in instructional time allotted to teach history, there has been an increase in politically correct material in history education. Senate Bill 48, which took effect January 1, 2012, requires that the California Education Code for social studies include the "role and contributions of lesbian, gay, bisexual and transgender Americans...to the total development of California and the United States."

As with many liberal ideas, parts of this new law, at first glance, seem fair and reasonable. The problem with the politically correct history...as in SB48, however, is that it has a point of view it wants to advance. History should be as fair and impartial as possible.

Historian Francis Parkman (1823–1893) wrote, "Faithfulness to the truth of history involves far more than research, however patient and scrupulous, into special facts. Such facts may be detailed with the most minute exactness, and yet the narrative, taken as a whole, may be unmeaning or untrue."

Parkman believed the historian should act as a spectator, an observer, to what occurred. SB48 and teaching a politically correct version of history, makes it even harder to be impartial...because it is history with an agenda. This can turn history into propaganda.

This politically correct approach to history started gaining increased public recognition in 1976 with the first observance of Black History Month. In 1981 Congress passed a resolution recognizing Women's History Week; the trend has continued.

The problem with specifically recognizing African Americans, women and other particular groups is that it turns history into advocacy. This skews reality. For instance, anti-slavery advocate Frederick Douglass was a remarkable man. His life is an inspirational testament to the human spirit, but when school texts give as much space to his story as they do to James Madison's, that is not an equal representation of each man's contribution to the United States.

In one of the social studies texts used in a local school, the writers, most willing to meet a requirement of including contributions of women, included the biblical story of Esther. Aside from the fact that there is considerable debate about the validity of the whole account, the version used was slanted to show Esther as a queen, not a pretty harem girl who managed to win the king's favor. These are only two of the sort of problems that can occur when government decides what to incorporate in teaching history.

The requirements of SB48 carry a potential for more unintended consequences than the similar treatment of other groups. Whether someone is black or a woman is pretty is obvious, but it is not always easy to know who is or was a LGBT (lesbian, gay, bisexual and transgender) individual.

Would future texts then include men such as Leonardo da Vinci or Abraham Lincoln in such a group? While neither man admitted to such a status, both were rumored to have been a part of it...at least by some.

Furthermore: What about people in cultures with an entirely different attitude toward sexuality? Ancient Greeks, from Socrates to Alexander the Great, lived in a culture that encouraged behavior now deemed gay. It could very well have been possible that in a different setting their lifestyles would not have been the same. To include them in the LGBT group, as defined by modern American culture, would be as unfair.

While proponents of SB48 argue that this law will make LGBT individuals feel better about themselves and decrease the bullying of such students, that shouldn't be the goal of teaching history. A person's race, gender or sexual preferences should not be criteria for inclusion in school's history texts...but rather what they personally accomplished.

Perhaps we would be better served if courses teaching the contributions of various ethnic groups and/or the sexual orientations of those therein...had the requirement of passing American History and World Geography before being introduced to those subjects in our educational systems.

Martin Luther King and Queen Elizabeth I deserve recognition because of what they did, not what they were.

In the limited teaching time available, history shouldn't be used to forward agendas of various groups. It is another step down that slippery slope that has the potential to become state-supported propaganda.

We all know, or should know...by now, there is an unacknowledged...fundamental disconnect in the direction that our public schools have been heading for decades. It has become nothing more than a "dog and pony show" orchestrated by the unions and our ever-expanding...self-serving government.

I read an article today reporting how Dohn Community High School in Cincinnati recently initiated a program that pays students to come to class and stay out of trouble. Seniors get $25 a week, and underclassmen $10. Similar payouts on a more-limited scale have been tried in Washington, D.C., and Camden, New Jersey.

Schools nationwide have employed incentive rewards, of one kind or another, to encourage attendance for a number of years now. But my question is, "What is the perceived value of something that you can't even give away for free, but have to pay people to take?" The answer is, not very much.

Sadly, that is how education is viewed by far too many in our population today. A free public education as envisioned by men like Thomas Jefferson was a noble idea. While there are and have always been problems with public education, for a long time it achieved pretty much what it was designed to do.

Most public school systems enacted by the states during the 19th century drew heavily on Thomas Jefferson's writings. Jefferson believed that attendance should be voluntary, that basic or primary education be limited, and that history should be emphasized in order to make students better future citizens.

Jefferson's belief that public education be voluntary was pragmatic. He wrote, "It is better to tolerate that rare instance of a parent refusing to let his child be educated, than to shock the common feelings by a forcible transportation and education of the infant against the will of his father."

This goes to the question of motivation. Students in our public schools realize that they can get by just fine without learning all the things the politicians have decided they should learn. Coupling this with the stripping away of the ability of teachers to enforce discipline in their classrooms, there is little wonder so many schools are chaotic to the point of being dysfunctional.

Jefferson also believed that basic education should be limited and with specific objectives. Teachers today are mandated to teach so much that there is no way all the "required" subjects can be given sufficient attention. There is literally not enough time in the school day to teach all the bureaucrats' demands, let alone teach it well to students who don't want to be there in the first place. If all students were given basic instruction in reading, writing and math, and then only those who were both able and willing advanced to higher levels of education, as Jefferson envisioned, we might have a public school system that works.

A final point of Jefferson's that I would like to highlight was his opinion that teaching history was important. He envisioned history being taught as part of the reading instruction. That's not how it is done in public schools today, and judging by whom we elect and what we vote for...the results would indicate the methods we've been using aren't working very well.

Our political leaders have lost sight of what public education should be and are legislating away any chance classroom teachers have to achieve the impossible results they demand. Paying students to attend school means that the system has failed to convince them that their education is worthwhile. If preparing our children for the future is paramount to the survival of our society, we are in jeopardy.

> "He who controls the present, controls the past. He who controls the past, controls the future."
>
> George Orwell

CHAPTER 13

"The pundits like to slice and dice our country into red states and blue states." This was Obama's opening salvo at the 2004 Democratic Convention and he was using it to position himself to become America's first "post-racial president"...bringing harmony and continuity to our country.

This is the man who sprang from nowhere with that 2004 convention speech declaring that we're "not a black and white America, a Latino America nor an Asian America, we're the United States of America." Of course that was then...today, we are becoming more and more tribal as we quarrel over our diversities...even as we're being exploited for political advantages. It makes a mockery of Obama's pose as the great "transcender," unifier, and healer of divisions...he is in fact, the most divisive president America has known. Obama is just the man to fulfill Al Gore's famous "mistranslation" of our national motto: Out of one, many.

The ever-changing face of America...I hardly recognize her today. I know the process has been occurring, incrementally for a long time...but it's only recently that the transformation blindsided me with all the subtlety of a train wreck. It was in my face the whole time and I didn't see it coming; a stealth like encroachment of many abstract components advancing from all directions...like a metastasizing cancer. I fear our country, as we knew it...has been irreparably changed.

I'm not talking about the oddities and/or the general unsightliness of our populace with their "look at me"... I'm current, mentality. Of course, the times are always changing...and the tattoo world is an excellent example. Less than a century ago, many of today's unemployed, heavily inked men and women could have gotten jobs with traveling circuses. Now, they hardly get a glance. We have become a developing "New World Order" circus.

Our "ringmaster" needs an additional four years to complete his agenda, and he will say or do whatever it takes to subjugate our American way-of-life.

Among those who have been disappointed by Obama, none are more painfully disappointed than those who saw his election as being a movement toward a "post-racial society."

Like so many other expectations that so many people projected onto this little-known man who suddenly burst onto the political scene, the expectation of movement toward a post-racial society had not a speck of hard evidence behind it...and all too many ignored indications of the very opposite, including his two decades of association with the hate mongering Reverend Jeremiah Wright.

Those "people of good will" who want to replace the racism of the past with a post-racial society have too often overlooked the fact that there are others, who instead...want to put racism under new management, to have reverse discrimination as racial payback for past injustices.

Attorney General Eric Holder became a key figure epitomizing the view that government's role in racial matters was not to be an impartial dispenser of equal justice for all, but to be a racial partisan and an organ of racial payback. He has been too politically savvy to say that in so many words, but his actions have spoken far louder than words.

The case that first gave the general public a glimpse of Attorney General Holder's views and values was one in which young black thugs outside a voting site in Philadelphia were televised intimidating white voters. When this episode was broadcast, it produced public outrage.

Although the Department of Justice's prosecution of these thugs began in the last days of the Bush administration, and the defendants had offered no legal defense, the case was dropped by the Justice Department after Eric Holder took over. One of the lawyers who was prosecuting that case resigned in protest.

That lawyer, J. Christian Adams...has now written a book entitled, "Injustice: Exposing the Racial Agenda of the Obama Justice Department." It is both thought provoking and shocking in regard to what it reveals about the inner workings of the civil rights division of the Department of Justice.

As bad as the Justice Department's decision was to drop that particular case (which it had already won in court), this book makes it painfully clear this was just the proverbial tip of the iceberg.

Despite the efforts of some in the media and in politics

to depict the voter intimidation in Philadelphia as just an isolated incident involving a few thugs at one voting place, former United States Attorney Adams shows these thugs were in fact part of a nationwide organization doing similar things elsewhere.

Moreover, the civil rights division of the Justice Department has turned the same blind eye to similar voter intimidation and corruption of the voting process by other people and organizations in additional cities and states; as long as those being victimized were white and the victimizers were black.

This is all spelled out in detail, naming names and places, not only among those in the country at large, but also among those officials of the Justice Department who turned its role of protecting the civil rights of all Americans into a policy of racial partisanship and racial payback.

The widespread, organized and systematic corruption of the voting process revealed by the author of "Injustice" is on a scale that can swing not only local but national elections, including the up-coming 2012 elections. The Department of Justice under Attorney General Eric Holder has ignored blatant evidence of voter fraud, and actively suppressed those United States Attorneys in its own ranks who have tried to stop such fraud.

Even in counties where the number of votes cast exceeds the number of people legally entitled to vote, Eric Holder's Justice Department sees no evil, hears no evil and speaks no evil...if the end result is the election of black Democrats. It has become the mirror image of the old Jim Crow South.

"Injustice" is an enormously eye-opening book that makes it painfully clear, where racial issues are concerned, the Department of Justice has become the Department of Payback. A post-racial society is the last thing that Holder and Obama are pursuing.

But there's more, I'm flabbergasted in an era when it takes a photo ID to purchase a television on a credit card or even to rent a video...that anyone would think twice about asking a voter to produce identification.

When anyone who doesn't have a driver's license can get a government photo identification card for free, exactly what barrier exists to anyone's entry into the voting arena? How many people took advantage of the not only free photo IDs but also free rides to pick them up when South Carolina required photo identification last year? The DMV said about 22 people asked for and got a free ride.

As I write this, voting is wrapping up in New Hampshire's primary. I'll go out on a limb and make a wild guess that less than half the eligible voters will even bother casting votes...and this when they are the only ones in the nation doing it, their chance to shine with the media giving them the spotlight.

Who really thinks having voter identification discourages anyone from casting a secret ballot? No, really...who does? The real suspicion is that if people are required to show proof that they are who they say they are, it will be more difficult to cast fraudulent ballots.

In Illinois lawmakers required people to present government-issued identification to purchase substances such as drain cleaner. But they rejected an ID requirement for voters at polling places.

Government's misguided over-reacting to "protect" people from odd, once-in-a-lifetime incidents is often "kneejerkingly" too quick. But to protect the safety of the ballot box, the "powers that be" aren't nearly as quick on the trigger.

Findings from the National Center for Public Policy Research: "The new Illinois law that tracks the sale of Drano was motivated by concerns over a single incident; while there are many instances of documented voter fraud all over the nation in just the past few years. Voter fraud in Illinois in 1960 may have influenced the presidential election."

If people must provide a government-issued ID to unclog their drains, they certainly should do the same for the very important task of selecting their elected leaders.

The most consequential election in our lifetime is still 10 months away, but it's clear from the Obama administration's order halting South Carolina's new photo ID law that the Democrats have already brought a gun to a fistfight.

How else to describe this naked assault on the right of a state to create minimal requirements to curb voter fraud!

On December 23, Assistant Attorney General Thomas E. Perez sent a letter ordering South Carolina to stop enforcing its voter photo ID law. Mr. Perez, who heads the Civil Rights Division that dropped the charges against the New Black Panther Party for intimidating white voters in Philadelphia in 2008, said South Carolina's law would disenfranchise thousands of minority voters.

Refresher course in history: On February 29, 1968, President Lyndon B. Johnson's National Advisory Commission on Civil Disorders (also known as the Kerner Commission) warned that racism was causing America to move "toward two societies, one black, one white... separate and unequal."

Today, I would suggest the once "black/white" disconnect has splintered into an array of multiple shades of ethnicities and customs as our country has become more and more diverse. I would also propose that the big driver for the growing wedge between groups is...in part, because of the divisiveness of the over used...but politically correct term, "Racist." It carries tremendous political clout...and there is no satisfactory response to the unsubstantiated allegation...especially if you're white. Our country has not been this divided since the Civil War!

It's blatantly apparent that "Eric Holder's agency" is using its clout to influence the direction of the nation's up-coming election in an effort to assure Obama's re-election in November.

Information indicates that Eric Holder's actions were squarely behind the ATF (Bureau of Alcohol, Tobacco and Firearms) operation known as "Fast and Furious," which orchestrated the delivery of almost 2,000 weapons to Mexican drug cartels.

The weapons deal was setup with "straw buyers" and even videotaped. Smuggled United States weapons from this operation, described as mostly semi-automatic versions of military weapons like the AK-47, were later used in the shooting deaths of two United States federal agents. Border Patrol Agent Brian Terry and Special Agent Jaime Zapata died from those weapons.

Holder had openly proclaimed his connection to the operation in April, 2009 during a publicized speech in Mexico, but later told an investigative Congressional

Committee in May 2011, "I probably heard about Fast and Furious...for the first time, in the last few weeks."

He then proclaimed that the committee was trying to get at Obama through him because, "We're both African Americans."

The natural tendency of every government is to grow steadily worse...that is, to grow more satisfactory to those who constitute it and less satisfactory to those who are expected to support it.

> "The urge to save humanity is almost always
> a false front for the urge to rule."

H. L. Mencken

Chapter 14

We're currently just a few weeks into the Trayvon Martin killing and what little we know...for sure, can be summarized as follows: It happened at night when Martin, returning from a local convenience store to the home of his father's girlfriend, caught the attention of a (by most accounts self-appointed) neighborhood watchman, George Zimmerman. Zimmerman phoned the police to report a suspicious person, pursued Martin on foot, apparently got into a physical altercation with him, and ended up firing a fatal round into Martin's chest... in what he claims was an act of self-defense.

The available details are scant...and the interpretative possibilities are wide-ranging. Zimmerman's most ferocious critics allege outright racism, to the point of trying to construe an unintelligible remark from his call to the police as a racial slur (the audio is so badly garbled that it's virtually impossible to hear what he's saying). His defenders, meanwhile, have suggested that Martin may have initiated the physical confrontation, dropping Zimmerman to the ground with a punch and repeatedly slamming his head against the sidewalk.

Yet despite the many uncertainties and ambiguities

the case presents, the media has already come to its conclusion: that Martin's death represented a racial flashpoint for America. Abject stupidity has been the result. MSNBC's Andrea Mitchell compared the incident to the grisly 1955 murder of 14-year old Emmett Till in Mississippi, a crime that was both premeditated and explicitly driven by racial hate. Obama, never missing a chance to propound the belief that we are all just satellites in his orbit, declared in the White House Rose Garden, "If I had a son, he'd look like Trayvon," as if the injustice he intuited was compounded because it befell someone fortunate enough to resemble him. Geraldo Rivera speculated on Fox News that the fact that Martin wore a hoodie was "as much responsible for his death as George Zimmerman was," despite the fact that Zimmerman mentioned the item of clothing in his call to police only once and without editorializing...and then only in response to a direct question from the operator about what Martin was wearing.

It's pathetic watching the prime-time mainstream media whip up the Trayvon Martin case to dangerous levels. The media is exploiting the terrible death of Martin by convicting the man who shot him...on television, before all the facts are on the table.

What would happen if the Florida special prosecutor decided there is not enough evidence to prosecute Zimmerman? It could, because Florida's complicated "stand-your-ground" law has muddled the case. MSNBC, and CNN to some extent, have a vested interest in seeing Zimmerman punished because they have already found him guilty on the air. So they are not going to respect any verdict but guilty.

As a result, if those entities tell the American public that a racial injustice has been perpetrated...due to the lack of a conviction, we could very well be seeing the same level of street violence that we saw in the Rodney King case. The 1992 riots in Los Angeles, reported that 58 people were killed and $1 billion in damage was done. That absolutely could happen in the Trayvon Martin case.

Then of course, the race hustlers (Sharpton and Jackson) showed up like Johnny on the spot...leading the charge to convict Zimmerman and revving up the troops. "This is not about self-defense. This is about a man deciding somebody, based on who he was, was a suspect and that he would take matters into his own hands. If Zimmerman is not arrested in Trayvon's killing, we will call for an escalation of peaceful civil disobedience and economic sanctions," Sharpton said.

Pundits who have no clue what happened that night are putting innocent people in danger by commentary based on emotion, not facts. No media observer knows exactly what happened the night Trayvon Martin was killed. Yet there they are, spreading unsupported accusations all over the place, exploiting the death of a young man, and inciting violence against the system.

Trayvon's dad, Tracy Martin, pointed to racial profiling... and the circumstantial evidence does point to racial profiling by Mr. Zimmerman, but that is not a proven fact.

The media seems to have an inherent bias against the quiet, solemn attitude that this story should merit. They instead imagine that by elevating the case of Trayvon Martin to metaphor status...for contentious political issues, they are somehow honoring the dead, and finding meaning where there is otherwise the chaos of ambiguity. In reality, they are diminishing the individual's life by subverting it to the needs of an endless news cycle that will forget them as soon as their stories grow stale. The victim, Trayvon Martin was not a martyr for American race relations. His life was simply cut short for reasons we don't yet (and may never) understand. If the media has nothing constructive to say about the facts, which it is becoming increasingly apparent in this case...it would be far better for them to remain silent, leaving the deceased to the peace of the grave.

Right now, there just isn't enough known about the circumstances surrounding the fatal shooting. If evidence emerges that Zimmerman's actions were not justified, he should be prosecuted and punished; however, there's a larger issue that few people understand or have the courage to acknowledge, namely that black and young has become synonymous with crime and, hence, suspicion; to make that connection does not make one a racist. Let's look at it.

Twelve years ago, a black Washington, D.C. commissioner warned cabbies, most of who were black, against picking up dangerous-looking passengers. She described "dangerous-looking" as "young black guys"...with shirttails hanging down longer than their coats, baggy pants and unlaced tennis shoes. She also warned cabbies to stay away from low-income black neighborhoods. Did that make the D.C. commissioner a racist?

In some cities, such as St. Louis, black pizza deliverers have complained about having to deliver pizzas to certain black neighborhoods, including neighborhoods in which they live. Are they racists?

Jesse Jackson once remarked, "There is nothing more painful for me at this stage of my life than to be walking down the street at night and hear footsteps coming up behind me, causing me to start thinking about being robbed...and then looking around and seeing a white individual and feeling relieved." Does that make Jackson a racist?

The former Charleston, South Carolina, black chief of police, Reuben Greenberg, said the problem facing black America is not racial profiling. He said, "The greatest problem in the black community is the tolerance for high levels of criminality." Former Los Angeles black police chief, Bernard Parks, defending racial profiling...said, "It's not the fault of the police when they stop minority males or put them in jail. It's the fault of the minority males for committing the crime. In my mind, it is not a great revelation that if officers are looking for criminal activity, they're going to look at the kind of people who are listed on crime reports." Are former police Chiefs Greenberg and Parks racist?

According to the Uniform Crime Report for 2009, among people 18 or younger, blacks were charged with 58 percent of the murders and non-negligent manslaughters, 67 percent of robberies, 42 percent of aggravated assaults and 43 percent of auto thefts. As for the murders, more than 90 percent of the time, their victims were black (but we never hear about Sharpton, Jackson or the media seeking justice for any of these black men...because there's no political gain). These statistics, showing a strong interconnection among race, youth and crime, are a far better explanation for racial profiling and suspicion than simple racism.

Everything about the Trayvon Martin case is a matter of contention. But about this, though, there should be no doubt: If Martin had been shot by a black classmate, if he had been caught in a random crossfire, if he had looked at a gang member the wrong way, his death would have been relegated to the back pages of the local newspaper. Not a cause, not even a curiosity...just another dead young black man.

Jesse Jackson is right that "blacks are under attack." According to a 2005 FBI report, blacks accounted for 13 percent of the population and 49 percent of all homicide victims. In 93 percent of the cases, the killer was black. Half of the victims were ages 17 to 29. That works out to 4,000 murders of young blacks in one year, overwhelmingly at the hands of other blacks. There is no comparable epidemic of any other ethnicity shooting young black men. Nor is there an epidemic of cops shooting young black men. In New York City, there were nine civilian victims of police gunfire last year, whereas there were several hundred black homicide victims in the city, almost all shot by other blacks or Hispanics...and none of them were given substantial press coverage.

A supposedly racially motivated killing, though, revs up the outrage machine in a way the routine murder of young blacks doesn't. Cable-TV outlets get to host fiery debates. Chin-stroking commentators get to urge more "dialogue." Black leaders get to relive the glory of a civil-rights cause that won its major victories decades ago when it took real courage to be on the front lines.

An injustice may well have been done in the handling of the Martin shooting, but let's not fool ourselves. Zimmerman could be arrested, convicted and hanged tomorrow, and it will have no effect on the lives of young black people in communities beset by social disorder.

Whatever happens to Zimmerman, the drip-drip of spilled blood will continue, all but ignored except in the police blotter. In America, the lives of young black people are cheap, unless they happen to fit the progressive's agenda.

Black Americans have spoken out against racial profiling by police. They've been insulted by store personnel who might give them extra scrutiny. There's the insult of the sound of a car door being locked when a black approaches. It's insulting to have taxi drivers pass up a black person and pick up white person down the street. In a similar vein, I'm sure that a law-abiding Muslim is insulted when given extra scrutiny at airports or listening to Fox News reporter Juan Williams, who was fired by National Public Radio in 2010 for publicly saying that he gets nervous when he sees people on a plane with clothing that identifies them as Muslim. Blacks and Muslims who face the insults of being profiled might direct their anger toward those who've made blacks and crime synonymous and terrorism and Muslims synonymous.

For most blacks to own up to the high crime rate among blacks is a source of considerable discomfort. Beyond that, it creates suspicions and resentment, which are destructive to good race relations, and it's devastating to the black community, which is its primary victim.

God would never racially profile, because he knows everything, including who is a criminal or terrorist. We humans are not gods; therefore, we must often base our decisions on guesses and hunches. It turns out that easily observed physical characteristics, such as race, are highly interconnected with other characteristics less easily observed.

The allegation of racism is a powerful political tool... and usually directed at whites. The term is a catchall facilitator for not only perpetuating, but also growing the myth that blacks are still enslaved by whites holding them back. This is not meant as a blanket statement...but there is a segment that still refuses to take responsibility for its existence.

We've all heard the statement, "minorities and women are encouraged to apply." It is usually followed, in close proximity by...the statement, "our institution does not discriminate on the basis of race." The two statements cannot be reconciled by logic. But of course, logic is considered a form of white oppression. Nor can those hiring statements be validated empirically. Not all minorities are encouraged: Orthodox Jews are not encouraged, white Mormons are not encouraged and neither are white-Hispanics. The fact that "minorities" really means "black" renders the second statement even less credible than the first. We really discriminate when we take affirmative action against discrimination.

The practice of establishing certain "preferred" minorities has been going on for a very long time. But, I had never really thought about the concept...or the scope, of such an abstract, self-serving misdirection of cultural and public strategy, until I heard the following question about the Zimmerman/Martin controversy: "What exactly is a white-Hispanic (a term used by the race hustlers at the height of the standoff)?" The response was, "It is a pathetic attempt to say that blacks are the only legitimate minority in America."

Make no mistake about it; the issue in George Zimmerman's case is not whether he had a right to shoot Trayvon Martin. It is the future of how race will be viewed in America. That is why Jesse Jackson and Al Sharpton are clinging to the Martin controversy.

In their struggle to maintain their "preferred" racial minority status and its accompanying affirmative action and other perks, race hustlers like Jackson and Sharpton regularly invoke the one-drop rule. The one-drop rule states that anyone who has even a drop of black blood is considered black. White racists in the South once used the rule. They thought that anyone who had a drop of black blood was contaminated, so to speak. Just a drop of black blood made them both intellectually and morally inferior.

Now race hustlers are using the one-drop rule to advance their own political agenda. Given that half of black pregnancies end in abortion, Jesse Jackson and his ilk must have some means of keeping their numbers and corresponding political influence from dwindling.

Of course, the one-drop rule operates differently with respect to Hispanics. Black civil rights leaders now want to say that having a single drop of white blood means you are white, not Hispanic. The reason for this is obvious, open-border immigration has made Hispanics the largest minority in America...numerically, if not politically, speaking.

It is also worth noting that these Hispanic immigrants are often Roman Catholic. That means they are less likely to abort their children than someone who practices black liberation theology. It helps explain why Hispanics are now 15 percent of the United States population while blacks constitute only 12 percent. This gradual displacement of blacks as America's preferred minority is producing a powder keg of racial tension in Florida and throughout America.

Racism is cultivated and marketed...front and center, by people like Jackson, Sharpton, the liberal mainstream media and politicians. All have a vested interest in keeping racism alive and well...and on Uncle Sam's plantation.

Perhaps the blacks will eventually figure out that the real threat to young men like Trayvon Martin is not a white-Hispanic named George Zimmerman, but a white supremacist named Margaret Sanger.

For the progressive Democrats who take offense at being called racist (only white conservatives can be racist), I direct you to the National Black Republican Association's website, where Dr. Arleta King, Martin Luther King's niece, and many others explain the history of politics as it relates to black people.

Dr. Arleta King asserts that Martin Luther King was a Republican and his belief that individuals should be judged by their character...rather than their skin color, reflects conservative thinking. This organization exists to educate people to rise above the "nanny state" mentality and consider achieving self-reliance and personal responsibility as a way to attain equality.

I have learned much from this group's website in regard to black history and the effects of the political process from contributors who have risen far above the racist rhetoric of the likes of Jesse Jackson and Al Sharpton.

CHAPTER 15

The civilized behavior we have known in the past is slowly...but steadily, being trampled by today's fast moving impersonal world. The list of infractions is endless, but some just stand out: The anonymous "bloggers" with their more often than not, hateful rudeness, the overly aggressive drivers always challenging for that vacant-car-length of space between moving vehicles, the cell phone addicts' "anywhere...anytime" lack of consideration for those around them; all this and more...driven by an ever growing "me" mentality, evolving from...and around our destructive entitlement culture.

We have become a country of special interests and double standards. If you dislike a black person you're a racist, but if that same black person dislikes you...it's their 1st Amendment right. Public schools can teach that homosexuality is okay, but they better not use the word "God" in the process. An unborn child can be killed, but it's wrong to execute a mass murderer. We don't burn books in America, we just re-write them...and we got rid of the communists and socialists by renaming them progressives. But one of our biggest casualties has been the traditional role of responsible...adult parenting; that's when the old-school messages of self-reliance, responsibility, accountability and common sense began its relegation to the accumulating relics of a by-gone time. So with those values out of the way, the path to government dependence was an easy next step.

And of course our all-knowing and caring government has all the answers. It will first appoint a committee to determine who and what...when and where. The committee's findings will of course trigger another mind-numbing series of legislative bills designed to appease their constituency. They will then raise our taxes (those of us who actually still pay taxes), and tell everyone the problem has been solved so they can get back to their reelection campaigning.

History offers plenty of examples of life becoming far worse than it had been centuries earlier.

The biographer Plutarch, writing 500 years after the glories of classical Greece, lamented that in his time weeds grew amid the empty colonnades of the once-impressive Greek city-states.

In America, most would prefer to live in the Detroit of 1941 than the Detroit of 2011. The quality of today's air travel has regressed to the climate of yesterday's bus service.

In 2000, Greeks apparently assumed that they had struck it rich with their newfound money-laden European Union lenders...even though they certainly had not earned their new riches through increased productivity, the discovery of more natural resources, or greater collective investment and savings.

The brief Euro mirage has vanished. Life in Athens is zooming backward to the pre-EU days of the 1970s. Then, most imported goods were too expensive to buy, medical care was often pre-modern, and the city resembled more a Turkish Istanbul than a European Munich.

The United States should pay heed to Greece, since our own rendezvous with reality is rapidly approaching. The costs of servicing a growing national debt of more than $16 trillion are starting to squeeze out other budget expenditures. Americans are no longer affluent enough to borrow hundreds of billions of dollars to import oil, while we snub our noses at vast new oil and gas finds beneath our own soil and seas.

For 40 years Californian's have hiked taxes; grown their government; vastly expanded entitlements; put farmland, timberland and oil and gas lands off-limits; and opened their borders to millions of illegal immigrants. They apparently assumed they had inherited so much wealth from prior generations and that their state was so naturally rich, that a continually better life was their natural birthright.

It isn't. Now, as in Greece, the veneer of civilization is proving pretty thin in California. Hospitals no longer have the money to offer sophisticated long-term medical care to the indigent. Cities no longer have the funds to self-insure themselves from the accustomed barrage of monthly lawsuits. When thieves rip copper wire out of streetlights, the streets stay dark. Most state residents would rather go to the dentist these days than queue up and take a number at the Department of Motor Vehicles. Hospital emergency rooms neither have room nor act as if there's much of an emergency.

Traffic flows no better on most of the state's freeways than it did 40 years ago...and often much worse, given the crumbling infrastructure and increased traffic. Once excellent K-12 public schools now score near the bottom in nationwide tests. The California State University system keeps adding administrators to the point where they have almost matched the number of teachers, although half of the students who enter CSU need remedial reading and math. Despite millions of dollars in tutoring, half the students still don't graduate. The taxpayer is blamed in constant harangues for not "ponying" up more money, rather than administrators being faulted for a lack of reform.

In 1960 there were far fewer government officials, far fewer prisons, far fewer laws and far fewer lawyers... and yet the state was a far safer place than it is a half-century later. Technological progress...whether "iPhones" or "Xboxes"...can often accompany moral regress. There are not yet weeds in our cities, but those, too, may be coming.

The average Californian, like the average Greek, forgot that civilization is fragile. Its continuance requires respect for the law, tough-minded education, collective thrift, private investment, individual self-reliance, and common codes of behavior and civility...and should exempt no one from those rules. Such knowledge and patterns of civilized behavior, slowly accrued over centuries, can be lost in a *single generation*.

Any aware visitors to Athens...or Los Angeles, during the past decade could have observed conditions that just didn't appear quite right...and concluded that the situation could not continue on indefinitely...as it was. And so it has not...

> "The more corrupt the state, the more numerous the laws."
>
> Tacitus

CHAPTER 16

President John F. Kennedy's "Inaugural Address," including his most famous quote: "Ask not what your country can do for you; ask what you can do for your country."

Kennedy's speech and quote were inspired by Kahlil Gibran's article whose Arabic title translates as "The New Frontier." It said, "Are you a politician asking what your country can do for you, or a zealous one asking what you can do for your country? If you are the first, then you are a parasite; if the second, then you are an oasis in the desert." But Kennedy twisted its meaning dramatically.

Clearly, politicians who benefit by abusing their positions are parasites.

Kennedy's rhetoric, exclusively invoked on behalf of government initiatives, ignores their history of consistent failure. In contrast, nothing is more inspiring than what individuals can achieve, pursuing their own advancement in liberty, through peaceful, voluntary cooperation that respects the equal rights of others.

As economist Milton Friedman put it, "Neither half of the

statement expresses a relation between the citizen and his government that is worthy of the ideals of free men in a free society. The paternalistic 'what your country can do for you' implies that government is the patron, the citizen and the ward, a view that is at odds with the freeman's belief in his own responsibility for his own destiny. The organismic, 'what you can do for your country' implies the government is the master... the citizen, and the servant."

Americans need to recognize that "ask not what your country can do for you," beyond what advances the general welfare, is good advice, but to "ask what you can do for your country" twists our founding principles. In fact, Richard Nixon offered more useful instruction when he said, *"Let each of us ask not what government will do for me, but what can I do for myself."*

What we do for ourselves, in voluntary arrangements with others, is all we can be sure will actually benefit Americans.

Obama's recent State of the Union message would have made Chairman Mao, Ho Chi-Minh, Vladimir Lenin, Fidel Castro, Hugo Chavez and Nikita Khrushchev all proud, but most of all...Karl Marx. His equality policy comes right out of Marx's writings. It is the socialist dream of utopia...a chicken in every pot; everyone has the same as everyone else, with the exception of those in power.

Our government is in such turmoil today because a constitutional government cannot function under a socialist regime.

The more power government has, the less the people have. The country Obama wants does not help anyone up, it brings everyone down to the lowest level of living standards. Property rights do not exist. We will all work for the government under the guise of working for each other. The government elites are the only ones who reap the benefits from the work of the classes.

We must get back to constitutional government, restore (acknowledge it's continuing relevance) the 10th Amendment and come back to the government of the people, for the people and by the people.

I'm always fascinated when people attribute very high incomes to greed. Greed tells you what you want. If you have high income it's because other people are willing to pay it. And those "other people" who have been willing to pay it more and more often...are in "most cases" the politicians who are spending the taxpayers' money.

Focusing attention and attacks on people who have greater wealth generating capacity...whether based on race, class or whatever...has had counterproductive consequences, including tragedies written in the blood of millions. Whole totalitarian governments have risen to dictatorial power on the wings of envy and resentment ideologies. Intellectuals have all too often promoted these envy and resentment ideologies.

There are both psychic and material rewards for the intelligentsia in doing so, even when the supposed beneficiaries of these ideologies end up worse off. When you want to help people, you tell them the truth. When you want to help yourself, you tell them what they want to hear. Both politicians and intellectuals have made their choice.

There is a great threat to medical care in America from a small group of our fellow citizens. They are not the top 1 percent of the wealthy, but a group of elitists and their allies who see government power as the means to determine what every American is allowed to earn and keep. Control over medical care is central to their objective of imposing control over every detail of our lives.

The 1 percent of Americans who really threaten our freedom in medical care and everything else is a small but relentless cadre. They follow an ancient precedent; Plato thought that "philosopher kings" should rule us (the New York Times agrees).

They subsequently have taken the forms of inquisition interrogators, witch hunters, Leninist enforcers of the "dictatorship of the proletariat," fascist followers of "the leadership principle," and the modern and most-hideous manifestation...intellectuals. The latter range from moral exhibitionists in Hollywood to the political-correctness police teaching in universities.

By contrast, the top 1 percent of wealthy Americans pay at least one-third of the total income taxes...far more than their "fair share" by anyone's standards except those pursuing power over others. The wealthy spend their after-tax wealth on what they buy from the rest of us, or they invest it. That is far more beneficial to the economy than what the government would do with the money.

Last fall, a particular columnist acknowledged that our Medicare and Social Security taxes had, for several generations...purchased government bonds, and that Congress used the proceeds immediately on other things it deemed more important and/or whatever. This writer then complained that the "enemies" of Social Security do not want to "raise the income taxes that may be needed to honor that debt obligation."

Who were the real enemies in Congress, and what

obligations to taxpayers did they dismiss? And...what would they do with new taxes for more government medical care?

How stupid do these intellectuals really think we are? After a lifetime of paying Medicare and Social Security taxes, we learn that Congress has blown through that money and wants to tax us again to pay back what they spent elsewhere. That is towering, majestic contempt for the American taxpayer.

Americans should reject intellectuals who exhibit such contempt for their intelligence.

Our greatest defense is the United States Constitution, including the Bill of Rights. At some level, most Americans realize this. When any political elitist tells you he knows best what health care you and your physician should be forced to live with, make sure you tell him exactly what you think of that. When in doubt, just ask yourself, "What would a true American say?"

We must remain relentlessly on guard against the truly dangerous, the "1 percent"...and their foot soldiers camped out in public places. Do you want your medical care decisions left to you and your physician's judgment? Or do you want to turn your decisions over to those who would...rather than seeking gainful employment and/ or taking responsibility for their useless existence, use physical obstruction and intimidation to "occupy" and replace your judgment with theirs?

I once heard a reporter (attempting to make the common man look foolish) ask a rural American why many Americans are anti-intellectual. The well-spoken man answered in a matter-of-fact tone...he said, "It's because most intellectuals are anti-American."

But we should treasure those intellectuals who still sustain the values of the framers of the United States Constitution.

The American people should already have known that Obama's plan to lower health cost while expanding coverage and bureaucracy is a myth, a promise of something that never has been and never can be..."a bureaucracy that lowers costs in a free society." Either the costs go up or the free society goes away. "A historical truth."

C. S. Lewis warned us about people like the "we know what's best for you intellectuals." "Of all tyrannies, a tyranny sincerely exercised for the good of its victims may be the most oppressive. It would be better to live under robber barons than under omnipotent moral busybodies.

The robber baron's cruelty may sometimes sleep, his cupidity may at some point be satiated; but those who torment us for our own good will torment us without end for they do so with the approval of their own conscience."

CHAPTER 17

The United States is not alone in its skepticism that mankind contributes to global warming; a 2009 Gallup survey found that Denmark, the United Kingdom, Norway and the Netherlands were other countries where less than half of respondents blamed global warming on human activity. In the United States, 48 percent of those polled said man contributes to global warming... the same as the world's average, according to a 2011 Gallup poll.

But there's a stark difference of opinion when you look at who in the United States is responsible for that skepticism. The difference correlates not with education level but with political party affiliation. Surveys show that the two parties have roughly the same level of education.

Among Orange County Republicans polled, 69 percent say man <u>does not</u> contribute to global warming or that there is no global warming. Among Democrats here, 98 percent say man <u>does</u> contribute to global warming. These findings by the Orange County Political Pulse poll portray an even starker partisanship than shows up in a Gallup nationwide poll. Perhaps because Orange County Political Pulse participants signed up for the polling project and so may be more politically engaged and ideological than those randomly phoned by Gallup.

Even more striking: Among county Republicans, 44 percent say <u>no</u> global warming is taking place. Among Tea Party identifiers, 54 percent say there is <u>no</u> global warming. Among conservative Christians, 41 percent say there is <u>no</u> global warming, while 97 percent of those who identify as "progressive" Christians say there <u>is</u> global warming and man <u>is</u> contributing to it.

Skeptics point to the dissenting scientists, the disagreement on details among scientists, historical fluctuations in global temperatures and an alleged political agenda among those who promote the notion of man-made global warming, amongst other things.

Both sides of the partisan divide tend to take their positions based more on ideology and emotion than a thorough understanding of the facts. It doesn't surprise me that the majority of Liberals/Progressives have fallen in line like lemmings racing toward the cliff. After all, it must be true...the warning came from their party leaders...and was effectively delivered by Al Gore, who like many other politicians, felt he was exempt from walking the talk. The Republicans/conservatives...on the other hand, understand that our politicians are not always looking out for "our" best interest and/or desires and must be challenged on such life altering legislation. We should always remember that most impingements on human rights were facilitated under the guise of necessity.

"People come to their political beliefs through emotions, but they think they came to them through facts," said Peter Ditto, who specializes in social psychology and has a Ph.D. from Princeton. He also volunteered that even he can't process the scientific information about global warming effectively enough to make his own determination.

Those who insist that a fraction of a degree over a century and a half is evidence of global warming raging out of control aren't real keen on what would disprove their alarmist theory.

But one of the high priest gurus of the movement said this not too long ago. "Bottom line...the no upward trend has to continue for a total of 15 years before we get worried," according to an email sent by Professor Phil Jones of the University of East Anglia Climatic Research Unit.

First, isn't it revealing that a lack of warming would be something to "get worried" about? If global warming is a threat, wouldn't a lack of it be time to rejoice, not lament? Well, maybe unless your reputation and paycheck are dependent on warming increasing.

Let's take a look at that 15-year rule that Jones pretty much arbitrarily set as a standard.

An analysis by the Global Warming Policy Foundation of the newly released HadCRUT4 global temperature database shows that there has been no global warming in the past 15 years. That's using the alarmists' favorite temperature database, by the way.

An editorial signed by 16 prominent scientists in the Wall Street Journal takes sharp issue with calls for drastic action against global warming, asserting that the threat is far from "incontrovertible" as alarmists claim.

The scientists point to Nobel Prize-winning physicist Ivar Giaever, who resigned from the American Physical Society in September due to the organization's position that the evidence for global warming is "incontrovertible" and the threat requires "mitigating actions" to reduce greenhouse gas emissions.

In spite of multiple international campaigns to enforce the message that increasing amounts of the pollutant carbon dioxide will destroy civilization, large numbers of scientists, many very prominent, share the opinions of Dr. Giaever.

In the 22 years since the United Nation's Intergovernmental Panel on Climate Change began issuing projections, warming has consistently been less than predicted.

It has now become apparent that "computer models" have greatly exaggerated how much warming additional CO_2 can cause. Faced with this embarrassment, those promoting alarm have shifted their drumbeat from warming to weather extremes, to enable anything unusual that happens in our chaotic climate to be ascribed to CO_2.

Why then does the call for action against global warming persist? The scientists said, "Follow the money."

Alarmism also offers an excuse for governments to raise taxes, taxpayer-funded subsidies for businesses that understand how to work the political system, and a lure for big donations to charitable foundations promising to save the planet. Alarmism over climate is of great benefit to many, providing government funding for academic research and a reason for government bureaucracies to grow.

I've always thought that the state of California's war on global warming never really had much to do with the globe getting warmer. Rather, it's always been about control and money.

Now the pretense should be obvious to all. The nonpartisan Office of the Legislative Analyst reported last week on Governor Jerry Brown's intention to raise money from a carbon emission cap-and-trade scheme through the regulatory might of the California Air Resources Board, enabled by the arrogantly titled Global Warming Solutions Act, approved in 2006 as Assembly Bill 32.

The act, of course, will not reduce global warming, even if warming was caused by greenhouse gas emissions, a dubious claim at best. That's because developing nations like China and India in coming years will vastly increase their emissions, the natural byproduct of industrial growth, something they are fully committed to. Their increased output will vastly overwhelm whatever slight reductions California might be able to achieve.

California's proposed cap-and-trade scheme, essentially a tax on industrial emissions, is expected to generate as much as $14 billion a year, according to a recent report from the Legislative Analyst. For California that represents a huge bailout for a perennially pressured state budget projected to be billions in the red this year, and for years into the future unless new revenue is found.

The tax-and-spend legislators, who stand to be enriched through this scheme, must be delighted. The state controller also reported last week that the state's January revenues were $1.2 billion below what lawmakers optimistically had expected in their current budget.

Footnote:

This past year temperatures in some areas of Europe sank to minus 26.5, parts of the Black Sea froze near the Romanian coastline and rare snow fell on Croatian islands in the Adriatic Sea. Heathrow Airport cut around half of the 1,300 flights scheduled during a two-day period in April 2012, after snow and freezing temperatures hit much of England.

Government definition of cap-and-trade:

> A cap-and-trade system constrains the aggregate emissions of regulated sources by creating a limited number of tradable emission allowances, which emission sources must secure and surrender in number equal to their emissions.

> In an emissions trading or cap-and-trade scheme, a limit on access to a resource (the cap) is defined and then allocated among users in the form of permits. Compliance is established by comparing actual emissions with permits surrendered including any permits traded within the cap.

> Under a tradable permit system, an allowable overall level of pollution is established and allocated among firms in the form of permits. Firms that keep their emission levels below their allotted level may sell their surplus permits to other firms or use them to offset excess emissions in other parts of their facilities.

The "stated" overall goal of an emissions trading plan is to minimize the cost of meeting a set emissions target. The cap is an enforceable limit on emissions that is usually lowered over time...aiming towards a national emissions reduction target. In other systems a portion of all traded credits must be retired, causing a net reduction in emissions each time a trade occurs. In many cap-and-trade systems, organizations which do not pollute may also participate, thus environmental groups can purchase and retire allowances or credits and hence drive up the price of the remainder according to the law of demand. Corporations can also prematurely retire allowances by donating them to a nonprofit entity and then be eligible for a tax deduction.

After a cap has been set by a governmental political process, individual companies are free to choose how or if they will reduce their emissions. Failure to reduce emissions is often punishable by a further government regulatory mechanism, a fine that increases costs of production. Firms will choose the least-costly way to comply with the pollution regulation, which will lead to reductions where the least expensive solutions exist, while allowing emissions that are more expensive to reduce.

From my perspective the global warming theory was concocted as the all-encompassing umbrella to unite the people of the world. A common...worldwide, survival cause where past differences can be set aside in the interest of mankind's continued existence. It's one of the major steps in a long pathway leading to a new world order...and the universal redistribution of the world's wealth.

Our entitlement burden (welfare and ObamaCare...unless it's repealed) is on the verge of bankrupting America... and again, in the interest of redistributing the wealth. Worldwide, things are crazy in many ways...and not the least of which is the possibility of a global financial collapse. As big and influential as the global warming narrative was...a failure of the world's monetary/economic systems (they're all interconnected) would provide the catastrophic doom's day scenario necessary for the world to regroup and unite under "a new world order" banner.

I recently read an article by Klaus Schwab, founder of the World Economic Forum in Davos, Switzerland. Schwab commented that the current global economic crisis was a "transformational crisis" that could be useful in reshaping a new world.

One of the scarier quotes in his piece was from a professor Nouriel Roubini, who said the global banking system was "effectively insolvent."

The last time this happened was in 1933, forcing the federal government to ban private ownership of gold so it could be confiscated and used to satisfy the government's creditors.

That was the national bankruptcy that predicated the Great Depression, which allowed Franklin Delano Roosevelt's administration to ram through the socialist "New Deal" policies that economic historians say made the Depression both longer and deeper than it needed to be.

During the Depression, FDR had more or less unhindered ability to push through whatever socialist legislation he deemed necessary. People were in pain and willing to accept almost anything the government proposed if it would make the pain go away.

"One of the first things I would expect to see introduced, as a consequence of this 'transformational crisis,' is the elimination of cash as a medium of exchange. This is a step that governments and banks have been trying to take for almost two decades without success."

There are "some" good and logical reasons for the elimination of cash. It will essentially wipe out the cash dependent drug trade. It will remove the incentive behind most petty crimes. Paper money is dirty, spreads disease and it is expensive to print and expensive to handle.

Electronic money addresses all of these issues in a single stroke. The difficulty will be in the overcoming of public resistance to the idea. But desperate times call for desperate measures, as the saying goes, and when the times get desperate enough, public resistance will evaporate like summer rain.

Footnote:

Associated Press: Stockholm, Sweden was the first European country to introduce bank notes in 1661. Now it has come farther than most on the path toward getting rid of them. The banking community there is questioning the need to still be printing bank notes at all anymore. And if you're wondering, yes...*the banks stand to profit handsomely from the ever-increasing number of digital "transactions."*

The contours of such a society are starting to take shape in this high-tech nation, frustrating those who prefer coins and bills to digital money.

In most Swedish cities, public buses don't accept cash; tickets are prepaid or purchased with a cell phone text message. A small but growing number of businesses only take cards, and some bank offices...which make money on electronic transactions, have stopped handling cash altogether.

"There are towns where it isn't possible anymore to enter a bank and use cash, complained Curt Persson, chairman of Sweden's National Pensioners' Organization, and that's a real problem for elderly people in rural areas who don't have credit cards or don't know how to use them to withdraw cash."

Bills and coins represent only 3 percent of Sweden's economy, compared to an average of 9 percent in the Euro zone and 7 percent in the United States, according to the Bank for International Settlements, an umbrella organization for the world's central banks.

Most experts don't expect cash to disappear anytime soon, but that its proportion of the economy will continue to decline as more payment options become available. Before retiring as deputy governor of Sweden's central bank last year, Lars Nyberg said, "Like the crocodile, cash will survive but will be forced to accept that its habitat will continue to incrementally shrink until..."

"...and cause that as many as would not worship the image of the beast should be killed. And he causeth all, both small and great, rich and poor, free and slave, to receive a mark in their right hand, or in their foreheads; and that no man might buy or sell, save he that had the mark, or the name of the beast, or the number of his name." Revelation 13:15-17

Just wondering...

CHAPTER 18

"These days"...I often reflect back to my rural Arkansas roots remembering the unknowing innocence of my youth, wishing I didn't know now what the future holds for my children and grandchildren.

Growing up in the carefree 40s and 50s, we (the young and old) were oblivious to the bleak future already being planned for not only us, but also for the as of yet... unborn generations of Americans. The "powers that be" were already at work on their "New World Order"...under the United Nations' control.

Historical reference point below:

U.S. Congressional Record February 9, 1917, page 2947:

Congressman Calloway announced that the J.P. Morgan interests bought 25 of America's leading newspapers, and inserted their own editors, in order to control the media.

The CHAIRMAN: The Chair will recognize the gentleman from Texas, a member of the defense appropriations committee.

Mr. CALLAWAY: Mr. Chairman, I ask unanimous consent to insert in the Record a statement that I have of how the newspapers of this country have been handled by the munitions manufacturers.

The CHAIRMAN: The gentleman from Texas asks unanimous consent to extend his remarks in the Record by inserting a certain statement. Is there any objection?

The CHAIRMAN: Is there any objection?

There was no objection.

Mr. CALLAWAY: Mr. Chairman, under unanimous consent, I insert into the Record at this point a statement showing this combination of newspapers' goals, which explains their activity in the war matter, just discussed by the gentleman from Pennsylvania (Mr. MOORE):

"In March, 1915, the J.P. Morgan interests, the steel, ship building and powder interests and their subsidiary organizations, got together 12 men high up in the newspaper world and employed them to select the most influential newspapers in the United States and sufficient number of them to control generally the policy of the daily press in the United States.

These 12 men worked the problems out by selecting 179 newspapers, and then began, by an elimination process, to retain only those necessary for the purpose of controlling the general policy of the daily press throughout the country. They found it was only necessary to purchase the control of 25 of the greatest papers. The 25 papers were agreed upon; emissaries were sent to purchase the policy, national and international, of these papers; an agreement was reached; the policy of the papers was bought, to be paid for by the month; an editor was furnished for each paper to properly supervise and edit information regarding the questions of preparedness, militarism, financial policies and other things of national and international nature considered vital to the interests of the purchasers.

This contract is in existence at the present time, and it accounts for the news columns of the daily press of the country being filled with all sorts of preparedness arguments and misrepresentations as to the present condition of the United States Army and Navy, and the possibility and probability of the United States being attacked by foreign foes.

This policy also included the suppression of everything in opposition to the wishes of the interests served. The character of the stuff carried in the daily press throughout the country since March 1915 has conclusively demonstrated the effectiveness of this scheme. They have resorted to anything necessary to commercialize public sentiment and sandbag the National Congress into making extravagant and wasteful appropriations for the Army and Navy under false pretense that it was necessary. Their stock argument is that it is 'patriotism.' They are playing on every prejudice and passion of the American people."

The CHAIRMAN: So entered.

Growing up in my generation we were taught that those who attempted to abolish our national sovereignty and overthrow our Constitutional government were committing acts of treason. But long before my time there were forces at work to do exactly that...abolish our national sovereignty. Today, that force is commonly known as The Council on Foreign Relations (CFR).

If one group is effectively in control of national

governments and multinational corporations; promotes world government through control of media, foundation grants, and education; and controls and guides the issues of the day; then they control most options available. The Council on Foreign Relations (CFR), and the financial powers behind it, have done all these things, and promote the "New World Order," as they have for over seventy years.

The CFR is the promotional arm of the Ruling Elite in the United States of America. Most influential politicians, academics and media personalities are members, and the council uses its influence to infiltrate the New World Order into American life. Its "experts" write scholarly pieces to be used in decision making, the academics expound on the wisdom of a united world, and the media members disseminate the message.

To understand how the most influential people in America came to be members of an organization working purposefully for the overthrow of the Constitution and American sovereignty, we have to go back at least to the early 1900's, though the story begins much earlier (depending on your viewpoint and beliefs).

Many Americans, in a position to know...have attested to the fact that a ruling power elite does indeed control the United States government from behind the scenes. Felix Frankfurter, Justice of the Supreme Court (1939-1962), said: "The real rulers in Washington are invisible and exercise power from behind the scenes." In a letter to an associate dated November 21, 1933, President Franklin Roosevelt wrote, "The real truth of the matter is, as you and I know, that a financial element in the large centers has owned the government ever since the days of Andrew Jackson."

February 23, 1954, Senator William Jenner warned

in a speech: "Outwardly we have a Constitutional government. We have operating within our government and political system, another body representing another form of government, a bureaucratic elite which believes our Constitution is outmoded."

Baron M.A. Rothschild wrote, "Give me control over a nation's currency and I care not who makes its laws."

All that is needed to effectively control a government is to have control over the nation's money: a central bank with a monopoly over the supply of money and credit. This had already been done in Western Europe, with the creation of privately owned central banks such as the Bank of England.

The Bank of the United States (1816-36) was an early attempt at an American central bank, but was abolished by President Andrew Jackson because he believed it threatened the nation. He wrote: "The bold effort the present bank had made to control the government, the distress it had wantonly produced...are but premonitions of the fate that awaits the American people should they be deluded into a perpetuation of this institution or the establishment of another like it."

Thomas Jefferson wrote: "The Central Bank is an institution of the most deadly hostility existing against the principles and form of our Constitution. If the American people allow private banks to control the issuance of their currency, first by inflation and then by deflation, the banks and corporations that will grow up around them will deprive the people of all their property until their children will wake up homeless on the continent their fathers conquered."

The United States managed to do without a central bank until early in this century when Congress created a National Monetary Commission. Headed by Senator Nelson Aldrich, father-in-law of John D. Rockefeller, Jr., the Commission recommended creation of a central bank.

Though unconstitutional, the Federal Reserve Act was passed in December 1913; ostensibly to stabilize the economy, but as Lindberg had warned, the passage established the most gigantic trust on earth...an invisible government powered by money. The Great Depression and numerous recessions later, it is obvious the Federal Reserve produces inflation and federal debt whenever it desires, but not stability.

When the Federal Reserve Act was passed, the people of the United States did not perceive that a world banking system was being set up here. A super-state controlled by international bankers and industrialists...acting together to enslave the world. Every effort was made by the Fed to conceal its powers, but the truth was...the Fed had usurped the government.

Although called "Federal," the Federal Reserve is privately owned by member banks, makes its own policies, and is not subject to oversight by Congress or the President. As the overseer and supplier of reserves, the Fed gave banks access to public funds, which enhanced their lending capacity.

One of the most important powers given to the Fed was the right to buy and sell government securities, and provide loans to member banks so they might also purchase them. This provided another built-in mechanism for profit to the banks, if government debt was increased. All that was needed was a method to pay off the debt. This was accomplished through the passage of the income tax in 1913.

Since it was graduated, the tax would "soak the rich," but the rich had other plans, already devising a method of protecting their wealth. By the time the 16th Amendment had been approved by the states, the Rockefeller Foundation was in full operation. John D. not only avoided taxes by creating four great tax-exempt foundations; he used them as repositories for his "divested" interests, made his assets non-taxable so that they might be passed down through generations without estate and gift taxes. Each year the Rockefellers dumped up to half their incomes into their pet foundations and deducted the "donations" from their income tax.

With the means (the Federal Reserve) to loan enormous sums to the government, a method to repay the debt (income tax), and an escape from taxation for the wealthy and their foundations, all that remained was an excuse to borrow money. By some happy "coincidence," in 1914, World War I began, and after American participation national debt rose from $1 billion to $25 billion.

Woodrow Wilson was elected President in 1913, beating incumbent William Howard Taft, who had vowed to veto legislation establishing a central bank.

World War I produced both a large national debt, and huge profits for those who had backed Wilson. The Rockefellers were reported to have earned over $200 million during the war and Wilson backer Cleveland Dodge sold munitions to the allies, while J.P. Morgan loaned them hundreds of millions, with the protection of the United States' entry into the war.

While profit was certainly a motive, the war was also useful to justify the notion of world government. During the 1950s, government investigators examining the records of the Carnegie Endowment for International Peace, a longtime promoter of globalization, found that several years before the outbreak of World War I, the Carnegie trustees were planning to involve the United States in a general war, to set the stage for world government.

The main obstacle was that Americans did not want any involvement in European wars. Some kind of incident, such as the explosion of the battleship Maine, which provoked the Spanish American war, would have to be provided as provocation. This occurred when a German submarine sank the Lusitania, carrying 128 Americans on board and anti-German sentiment was aroused. When war was declared, United States propaganda portrayed all Germans as Huns and fanged serpents, and all Americans opposing the war as traitors.

What was not revealed at the time, however, was that the Lusitania was transporting war munitions to England, making it a legitimate target for the Germans. Even so, they had taken out large ads in the New York papers, asking that Americans not take passage on the ship.

It would seem that the Lusitania was deliberately sent, at considerably reduced speed, into an area where a U-boat was known to be waiting. Thus, even though Wilson had been reelected in 1916 with the slogan "He kept us out of war," America soon found itself fighting a European war. Actually, Colonel House had already negotiated a secret agreement with England, committing the United States to the conflict. It appears the American public had little say in the matter.

With the end of the war and the Versailles Treaty, which required severe war reparations from Germany, the way was paved for a leader in Germany...Hitler.

Wilson brought his famous "fourteen points," to the Paris Peace Conference with point fourteen being a proposal for a "general association of nations," which was to be the first step towards the goal of *One-World Government...the "League of Nations."*

It was later revealed that the League was not Wilson's idea. Not a single idea in the Covenant of the League was original with the President. Colonel House was the author of the Covenant, and Wilson had merely rewritten it to conform to his own phraseology.

The League of Nations was established, but it, and the plan for world government eventually failed because the United States Senate would not ratify the Versailles Treaty.

Pat Robertson, in "The New World Order," states that Colonel House, along with other internationalists, realized that America would not join any scheme for world government *"without a change in public opinion."*

The Council on Foreign Relations was incorporated as the American branch in New York on July 29, 1921. Founding members included Colonel House, and such potentates of international banking as J.P. Morgan, John D. Rockefeller, Paul Warburg, Otto Kahn, and Jacob Schiff...the same clique that had engineered the establishment of the Federal Reserve System.

Over time Morgan's influence was lost to the Rockefellers, who found that one-world government fit their philosophy of business well. As John D. Rockefeller, Sr. said, "Competition is a sin," and global monopoly fit their needs as they grew internationally.

As corporations went international, national monopolies could no longer protect their interests. What was needed was a one-world system of government controlled from behind the scenes. This had been the plan since the time of Colonel House, and to implement the plan, it was necessary to weaken the United States politically and economically.

During the 1920s, America enjoyed a decade of prosperity, fueled by the easy availability of credit. Between 1923 and 1929 the Federal Reserve expanded the money supply by sixty-two percent. When the stock market crashed, many small investors were ruined, but not "insiders." In March of 1929 Paul Warburg issued a tip the "Crash" was coming, and the largest investors got out of the market. But none dared to call it a conspiracy.

With their fortunes intact, they were able to buy companies for a fraction of their worth. Shares that had sold for a dollar might now cost a nickel, and the buying power, and wealth, of the rich increased enormously.

Louis McFadden, Chairman of the House Banking Committee declared: "It was not accidental. It was a carefully contrived occurrence. The international bankers sought to bring about a condition of despair here so that they might emerge as rulers of us all."

Curtis Dall, son-in-law of FDR and a syndicate manager for Lehman Brothers, stated: "It was the calculated 'shearing' of the public by the World-Money powers triggered by the planned sudden shortage of call money in the New York Market."

The Crash paved the way for the man Wall Street had groomed for the presidency, FDR. Portrayed as a "man of the little people," the reality was that Roosevelt's family had been involved in New York banking since the eighteenth century.

Frederic Delano, FDR's uncle, served on the original Federal Reserve Board. FDR attended Groton and Harvard, and in the 1920s worked on Wall Street, sitting on the board of directors of eleven different corporations.

Dall wrote of his father-in-law: "Most of his thoughts, his political 'ammunition' were carefully manufactured for him in advance by the CFR-One-World-Money group. Brilliantly...he exploded that prepared 'ammunition' in the middle of an unsuspecting target, the American people...and thus paid off and retained his internationalist political support."

Taking America off the gold standard in 1934, FDR opened the way to unrestrained money supply expansion, decades of inflation...and credit revenues for banks. Raising gold prices from $20 an ounce to $35, FDR and Treasury Secretary Henry Morgenthau, Jr. (son of a founding CFR member), gave international bankers huge profits.

FDR's most remembered program, the New Deal, could only be financed through heavy borrowing. In effect, those who had caused the Depression loaned America the money to recover from it. Then, through the National Recovery Administration, proposed by Bernard Baruch in 1930, they were put in charge of regulating the economy. FDR appointed Baruch disciple Hugh Johnson to run the NRA, assisted by CFR member Gerard Swope. With broad powers to regulate wages, prices, and working conditions, it was, as Herbert Hoover wrote in his memoirs: "Pure fascism, merely a remaking of Mussolini's corporate state." The Supreme Court eventually ruled the NRA unconstitutional.

Since 1934 almost every United States Secretary of State has been a CFR member; and all Secretaries of War or Defense, from Henry L. Stimson through Richard Cheney.

Most presidential candidates have been CFR members. President Truman, who was not a member, was advised by a group of "wise men," all six of whom were CFR members, according to Gary Allen. In 1952 and 1956, CFR Adlai Stevenson challenged CFR Eisenhower.

In 1960, it was CFR member Kennedy (who was probably killed because he had the courage not to go along with all their plans) and in 1972, CFR member Nixon. In 1964 the GOP stunned the Establishment by nominating its candidate over Nelson Rockefeller.

In 1976 we had Jimmy Carter, who was also a member of the Trilateral Commission, created by David Rockefeller and CFR members. Their goal entailed an economic linkage between Japan, Europe, and the United States that would manage the world's economy in a smooth and peaceful evolution of the global system. We have also had CFR director (1977–1979) George Bush, and last but not least, CFR member Bill Clinton.

They have all promoted the "New World Order," controlled by the United Nations. "The problem is that the present United Nations organization is actually the creation of the CFR and is housed on land in Manhattan donated to it by the family of current CFR chairman David Rockefeller," as Pat Robertson describes it.

Since that time the CFR and its friends in the mass media (largely controlled by CFR members), foundations, and other political groups have lobbied consistently to grant the United Nations more authority and power. Bush and the Gulf War were but one of the latest calls for a "New World Order."

Admiral Chester Ward, a member of the CFR for over a decade, became one of its harshest critics, revealing its inner workings in his 1975 book. In it he states,

"The most powerful cliques in these elitist groups have one objective in common, they want to bring about the surrender of the sovereignty and national independence of the United States."

Most members are one-world government ideologists whose long-term goals were officially summed up in the September, 1961 State Department Document 7277, adopted by the Nixon Administration: *"Elimination of all armed forces and armaments except those needed to maintain internal order within states and to furnish the United Nations with peace forces, by that time it (United Nations global government) would be so strong that no nation could challenge it."*

Within the CFR there exists a much smaller group but more powerful...made up of Wall Street international bankers and their key agents. Primarily, they want the world banking monopoly from whatever power ends up in control of the global government. This CFR faction is headed by the Rockefeller brothers, according to Ward.

What must be remembered is that this is not some lunatic-fringe group...these are members of one of the most powerful private organizations in the world; the people who determine and control American economic, social, political, and military policy. Members' influence and control extends to leaders in academia, public service, business, and the media, according to the CFR 1993 Annual Report.

The CFR states that it is host to many views; advocate of none, and it has no affiliation with the United States government. No, no affiliation at all, if you don't count... Council members elected president of the United States, dozens of other Council colleagues called to serve in cabinet and sub-cabinet positions described as Foreign Affairs positions along with many members of Congress, the Supreme Court, the Joint Chiefs, the Federal Reserve, and many other Federal bureaucrats.

They are not affiliated with government? They are the government, in effect!

One re-occurring view was stated in the 50th anniversary issue of "Foreign Affairs," the official publication of the CFR. In an article by Kingman Brewster, Jr., entitled Reflections on Our National Purpose, he states, "Our purpose should be to do away with our nationality, to take some risks in order to invite others to pool their sovereignty with ours."

These risks include disarming to the point where we would be helpless against the "peace-keeping" forces of a global U.N. government. We should happily surrender our sovereignty to the world government in the interests of the *world community.*"

Today we have the spectacle of Specialist 4 Michael New, a United States soldier in Germany who refuses to wear the uniform of the United Nations, facing an "administrative discharge." He states rightly that he swore an oath to defend the United States Constitution, not the United Nations. Many other Americans have taken that same oath, such as myself, and believe it is our sworn duty still to defend the Constitution, since an oath sworn before God must be fulfilled. (Why else do we swear to tell the truth in our courts, or when taking public office?) Is it a crime these days to actually believe in God and the oath that was taken?

Meanwhile, others who attempt to destroy the Constitution and our sovereignty are given honors and position. At least they are not hypocrites...only supremely arrogant.

In short, the "house of world order" will have to be built

from the bottom up rather than from the top down. An end run around national sovereignty, eroding it piece by piece, will accomplish much more than the old fashion assault...in the opinion of Richard N. Gardner, former Deputy Assistant Secretary of State in "Foreign Affairs," April 1974.

James Warburg, son of CFR founder Paul Warburg, and a member of FDR's brain trust, testified before the Senate Foreign Relations Committee on February 17, 1950, *"We shall have world government whether or not you like it... by conquest or consent."*

Was this an American speaking, or a dangerous lunatic? And who is this "We" who threatens to conquer us?

They are a group that actually has the power to do it, and is doing it every day, bit by bit.

CFR Members in the mass media, education, and the entertainment industry push their propaganda of "humanism" and *"world brotherhood."* We should all live in peace under a world government, and forget about such selfish things as nationalities and patriotism. We can solve our own problems. We don't need God, morals or values. It's all relative anyway, right? Because if we actually had some moral character and values, we might be able to discern that these people are actually evil.

The Bible says that the love of money is the root of all evil. These people are evil because they love money and power, and greed drives them to do anything to achieve their goals. They have lost all morality and conscience, and believe such concepts, as well as our Constitution, are "outdated."

That is insanity...to have more wealth than can be spent, and still it is never enough. They have to control governments, start wars, conspire to rule the world; lest the "common people" wake up to how they have gained their wealth, take it away from them, and demand that they pay the price for their crimes.

That is why they constantly pit us one against the other, with diversity, Affirmative Action, and other programs... black against white, men against women, rural against urban, ranchers against environmentalists, and on and on...lest we look in their direction.

We The People are held to a much higher standard. If we threaten the President or a public official, we are charged with a crime...yet the One-World-Gang can threaten the Constitution and the liberties of We The People, the sovereign rulers of this nation, and nothing is said or done.

Perhaps they do not fear what Man can do to them... they believe they have arranged everything, and their power and wealth will prevail in this world. However, those among them who have sworn an oath before God to uphold and defend the Constitution, the President, members of Congress, and the military...may find one day that they do indeed have something to fear.

There is much more to say about this group and their plans for America. Gary Allen, in "The Rockefeller File," states that they are behind the many regional government plans, which would abolish city, county, and state lines, leaving us at the mercy of federal bureaucrats, and behind the push for "land use controls." They want federal control of everything. Since they intend to control the federal government.

There are also the many allegations of involvement in gun running, drug smuggling, prostitution and sex slaves... and the many mysterious assassinations and "suicides" of witnesses and others who get too close to the truth... but that is another story.

This document may be freely distributed or quoted in any medium, provided credit is given to the author and The Courier. Copyright 1995

Author: William Blasé

The preceding article (by William Blasé) was edited and condensed for this book by: Richard McKenzie Neal.

The Council has been the subject of much debate due to the number of high-ranking government officials (along with world business leaders and prominent media figures) in its membership, its secrecy clauses, and the large number of aspects of American foreign policy that its members have been involved with, beginning with Wilson's Fourteen Points. Wilson's Fourteen Points speech was the first in which he suggested a worldwide security organization to prevent future world wars.

The John Birch Society believes that the CFR is "Guilty of conspiring with others to build a one-world government." In 1980, a conservative Democratic congressman from Georgia...Larry McDonald, the second head of the John Birch Society, introduced American Legion National Convention Resolution 773 to the House of Representatives calling for a congressional investigation into the Council on Foreign Relations, but nothing came from it.

Carroll Quigley claimed it was well known that there was an international conspiracy to bring about a one-world government. In "Tragedy and Hope," he based his analysis on un-sourced research in the papers of an Anglo-American elite organization that, he felt, secretly controlled the United States and United Kingdom governments through a series of Round Table Groups.

Critics assailed Quigley for his approval of the goals (not the tactics) of the Anglo-American elite while selectively using his information and analysis as evidence for their views. Speaking of Carroll Quigley, Rep. Larry McDonald said, "Sure we've been working it, sure we've been collaborating with communism, yes we're working with global accommodation, and yes we're working toward a world government. But the only thing I object to is that we've kept it a secret." CFR publications discuss "multilateralism" and global governance as well.

Is it just me, or is all this starting to sound a lot like "1984"...George Orwell's book written in 1949? In 1949 it would have made a great Twilight Zone movie, but today it's a good representation of how far America has drifted from the founding fathers' vision. Perhaps one day the History Channel will produce a documentary on the subject...and reveal how we went from the most powerful, free nation in the world to serfdom under the United Nations' flag.

> "None are more hopelessly enslaved, as those who falsely believe they are free."
>
> Johann Wolfgang Von Goethe

CHAPTER 19

There is no doubt in my mind that "in time" the global population will become an all-inclusive assemblage. It will be accomplished through the coordinated efforts of the political power brokers around the world. After 90-plus years the brew is beginning to simmer and if Doctor Frankenstein is able to manipulate a majority into giving him an additional four years...the "Beast" could become our new world.

The biggest fly in the ointment is the disarming of America. It was surprising to me to learn how many countries have already disarmed their citizens...under the guise of controlling the criminal element. I wasn't surprised to learn that those countries now have higher crime rates than the United States.

I found another tidbit of enlightening information while reading from my NRA Magazine: Last year America had 10.1 million United States deer hunters...and that's just accounting for the ones who are actually licensed. I dare say that would be the largest standing armed army in the world. Now you know why they want us disarmed. Just food for thought...

They want us disarmed because we pose a threat to their desire to control every aspect of our lives.

The United Nations maneuvers to create "Global Gun Control."

January 8, 2010

In October unbeknownst to most of us, Secretary of State Hillary Clinton announced the Obama administration would reverse the Bush administration's opposition to the United Nations' proposed International Small Arms Treaty. This will clear the way for the treaty to reach a vote by the United Nations' General Assembly. So what could this treaty require of its signatories? Well, here is a quick overview according to The National Association for Gun Rights:

If passed by the United Nations and ratified by the United States Senate, the United Nations' "Small Arms Treaty" would almost certainly force national governments to: Enact tougher licensing requirements, making law-abiding citizens cut through even more bureaucratic red tape just to own a firearm legally; confiscate and destroy all "unauthorized" civilian firearms (all firearms owned by the government are excluded, of course); ban the trade, sale and private ownership of all semi-automatic weapons; create an international gun registry, setting the stage for full-scale gun confiscation at some point in the future. And yes, it does sound a lot like Germany's gun controls leading up to Hitler's take over.

The Worldwide Gun Control Movement: The United Nations is holding a conference beginning this week in New York that ironically coincides with our national 4th of July holiday. It's ironic because those attending the conference want to do away with one of our most fundamental constitutional freedoms...the right to bear arms.

The stated goal of the conference is to eliminate trading in small arms, but the real goal is to advance a worldwide gun control movement that would ultimately supersede national laws, including our own Second Amendment. Many United Nations observers believe the conference will set the stage in coming years for an international gun control treaty.

Fortunately, United States gun owners have responded with an avalanche of letters to the American delegation to the conference, asking that none of our tax dollars be used to further United Nations anti-gun proposals. We cannot discount the growing power of international law, whether through the United Nations, the World Trade Organization, or the NAFTA and CAFTA treaties. Gun rights advocates must understand that the forces behind globalism are hostile toward our Constitution and national sovereignty in general. Our Second Amendment means nothing to United Nations officials.

Domestically, the gun control movement has lost momentum in recent years. The Democratic Party has been conspicuously silent on the issue in recent elections because they know it's a political loser. In the midst of declining public support for new gun laws, more and more states have adopted concealed-carry programs. The September 11th terrorist attacks and last summer's hurricanes only made matters worse for gun control proponents, as millions of Americans were starkly reminded that we cannot rely on government to protect us from criminals.

So it makes sense that perhaps the biggest threat to gun rights in America today comes not from domestic lawmakers, but from abroad.

For more than a decade the United Nations has waged a campaign to undermine Second Amendment rights in America. The United Nations' Secretary General Kofi Annan has called on members of the Security Council to address the "easy availability" of small arms and light weapons, by which he means all privately owned firearms. In response, the Security Council released a report calling for a comprehensive program of worldwide gun control, a report that admonishes the United States and praises the restrictive gun laws of Red China and France!

It's no surprise that United Nations officials dislike what they view as our gun culture. After all, these are the people who placed a huge anti-gun statue on American soil at United Nations' headquarters in New York. The statue depicts a pistol with the barrel tied into a knot, a not-too-subtle message aimed squarely at the United States.

They believe in global government, and armed people could stand in the way of their goals. They certainly don't care about our Constitution or the Second Amendment. The conflict between the United Nations' position on private ownership of firearms and our Second Amendment cannot be reconciled. How can we as a nation justify our membership in an organization that is actively hostile to one of our most fundamental constitutional rights? What if the United Nations decided that free speech was too inflammatory and should be restricted? Would we discard the First Amendment to comply with the United Nations' agenda?

The United Nations claims to serve human freedom and dignity, but gun control often serves as a gateway to tyranny. Tyrants from Hitler to Mao to Stalin have sought to disarm their own citizens, for the simple reason that unarmed people are easier to control. Our Founders, having just expelled the British army, knew that the right to bear arms serves as the guardian of every other right. This is the principle so often ignored by both sides in the gun control debate. Only armed citizens can resist a tyrannical government.

June 27, 2006

Dr. Ron Paul, a Republican member of Congress from Texas.

Second Amendment antagonists claim that the individual right to keep and bear arms is some sort of anachronism, no longer important since the days of the Redcoat.

Decades of sociological research refute that allegation, of course, demonstrating to the contrary that greater firearm possession by law-abiding citizens correlates with lower crime. Moreover, armed Korean shop owners successfully defended their lives and livelihoods from their rooftops during the 1992 Los Angeles riots, providing vivid contemporary illustration of that reality.

And now, Detroit provides just the latest evidence of the Second Amendment's continuing relevance.

Paradoxically, Detroit should by every measure provide a utopian liberal model. As the Mackinac Center's Jarrett Skorup points out, it is "a city where all the major economic planks of the statist or 'progressive' platform have been enacted." Detroit enforces a so-called "living wage" law much higher than the nationwide minimum wage for public employees and contractors. Its public school spending per pupil far exceeds the national average. Its public and private unions are exceedingly powerful presences. More broadly, its left-wing policies have earned it the nickname "the most liberal city in America," Mr. Skorup notes.

Instead of creating a utopia, however, those policies have led to disaster. Detroit was the wealthiest city in the United States per capita just 60 years ago, but now is the second poorest.

It is also now the second-most dangerous. Such are the real-world consequences of decades of "progressive" governance. In 2011 alone, homicides rose 10 percent to 344, even though the city's dramatic overall de-population continued. Unfortunately, the number of city police available to deter and respond also continues to fall. Just ten short years ago, Detroit claimed 5,000 police. Today there are fewer than 3,000.

Unsurprisingly, that decline in personnel has led to a dangerous increase in police response time. According to recent data, response time to priority calls averages 24 minutes, versus the nationwide average of under 10 minutes.

Unable to rely on a police force spread too thin, desperate Detroit citizens have therefore responded in the only way they can...by relying upon themselves. In a recent article entitled, "911 is a Joke," The Daily reported in harrowing detail how people have taken to self-defense:

Residents unable to rely on a dwindling police force to keep them safe, are fighting back against the criminal scourge on their own. And they're offering no apologies. "We got to have a little Old West up here in Detroit. That's what it's gonna take," Detroit resident Julia Brown told The Daily. The last time Brown, 73, called the Detroit police, they didn't show up until the next day. So she applied for a permit to carry a handgun and says she's prepared to use it against the young thugs who have taken over her neighborhood, burglarizing entire blocks, opening fire at will and terrorizing the elderly with impunity. "I don't intend to be one of their victims," said Brown, who has lived in Detroit since the late 1950s. "I'm planning on taking one out."

Reflecting that awakening, the number of justifiable self-defense homicides in Detroit increased 79 percent last year. To place that in a broader perspective, Detroit's rate of self-defense killings now exceeds the national average by 2,200 percent. "We don't hardly see police anymore," Detroit resident James Jackson said.

Meanwhile, violent crime rates continue to decline across the United States in jurisdictions that have relaxed firearm restrictions. That includes the cities of Chicago and Washington, D.C., whose draconian prohibitions were overturned in recent United States Supreme Court decisions. Like clockwork, anti-gun activists and liberal politicians predicted swift increases in crime. Instead, both cities saw declines.

We cannot know whether Detroit will merely constitute the latest illustration of the Second Amendment's continuing importance, or signal a future trend. As other cities, states and even the federal government confront budget crises similar to Detroit's, basic collective responsibilities like maintenance of civic order could conceivably be sacrificed in favor of growing entitlement constituencies.

We hope that will not occur. But if it does, the individual right to keep and bear arms remains our bulwark against the ever-present possibility of the breakdown in civic order.

The next time you see one of those media stories talking about the dire threat of "workplace violence," consider how the current administration is classifying some incidents.

It recently came to light that the Obama Defense

Department has classified the terrorist massacre of 13 service men and women by Major Nidal Hasan, a Muslim extremist, at Fort Hood, Texas, under the category of "workplace violence."

According to a Fox News report, Senator Susan Collins, R–Maine, blasted the Defense Department for depicting the shooting this way, suggesting that political correctness is being placed above the security of the nation's armed forces. In her letter, Collins said, "The documents attached illustrate how the Department is dealing with the threat of violent Islamist extremism in the context of a broader threat of workplace violence."

Unfortunately for law-abiding gun owners, such classification of a terrorist act also gives anti-gunners 13 more reasons to call for more restrictive gun control measures, rather than supporting anti-terrorist programs.

While delivering one of the liveliest and best-received speeches at the Conservative Political Action Conference in Washington, NRA Executive Vice President Wayne LaPierre said, "The president's low-key approach to gun rights during his first term has been a conspiracy to ensure re-election by lulling gun owners to sleep.

All the first term lip-service to gun owners is just part of a massive Obama conspiracy to deceive voters and hide his true intentions to destroy the Second Amendment during his second term. *It's well understood that to be a credible movement for constitutional change...and a credible social movement, that movement has to deny, in a sense, its ultimate goal.*

We see Obama's strategy crystal clear...get re-elected, and with no more elections to worry about, get busy dismantling and destroying our firearms' freedom, erase the Second Amendment from the Bill of Rights and excise it from the United States Constitution."

Mr. LaPierre went on to say that Obama's two Supreme Court appointees...Sonia Sotomayor and Elena Kagan, are "two of the most rabid anti-gun justices in history." He also accused Justice Ruth Bader Ginsburg of being a foe of gun rights.

And with the possibility of two or more Supreme Court justice positions opening during the next four years, the NRA official warned that gun ownership would be in jeopardy if Obama stays in office.

If we get one more justice like those three, the Second Amendment is finished and it will be the end of our freedom forever.

First they came for the Jews and I did not speak out, because I was not a Jew.

Then they came for the Communists and I did not speak out, because I was not a Communist.

Then they came for the trade unionists and I did not speak out, because I was not a trade unionist.

Then they came for me and there was no one left to speak out for me.

This reminded me of a documentary on the Holocaust Museum in Israel. There was a sign at the entrance with a quote that I wish I had written down verbatim, but it went something to the effect that people just laid down their freedoms, very few stood up and the government steam rolled the rest of their freedoms. It could happen again folks, do not be fooled!

Back to the United Nations: Agenda 21 is an action plan of the United Nations related to sustainable development and was an outcome of the United Nations Conference on Environment and Development (UNCED) held in Rio de Janeiro, Brazil, in 1992. It is a comprehensive blueprint of action to be taken globally, nationally, and locally by organizations of the United Nations, world governments, and major groups in every area in which humans directly affect the environment.

The full text of Agenda 21 was revealed at the conference, where 178 governments voted to adopt the program. The final text was the result of drafting, consultation, and negotiation beginning in 1989 and culminating at the two-week conference. The number 21 refers to an agenda for the 21st Century.

In 1997, the General Assembly of the United Nations held a special session to appraise progress on the implementation of Agenda 21. The Assembly recognized progress as 'uneven' and identified key trends including increasing globalization, widening inequalities in income and a continued deterioration of the global environment. A new General Assembly Resolution (S-19/2) promised further action.

The Johannesburg Plan of Implementation, agreed upon at the World Summit on Sustainable Development (Earth Summit 2002) affirmed United Nations commitment to 'full implementation' of Agenda 21, alongside achievement of the Millennium Development Goals and other international agreements.

There are groups in the United States opposed to Agenda 21, which includes Republicans and Democrats.

Some on the American right view Agenda 21 as a plan

to stealthily impose worldwide, centralized control over people, attacking private property and energy usage.

The Republican National Convention has adopted a resolution regarding Agenda 21 (approved January 13, 2012), which asserted that Agenda 21 "is a comprehensive plan of extreme environmentalism, social engineering, and global political control." According to the National Federation of Republican Assemblies, "it is a disregard for American freedom, private property rights, and a key player in the Leftist move toward a one world government. Agenda 21 assaults the very foundation of America."

Americans are so focused on Congress and Obama at the federal level of government right now that most are overlooking the socialism creeping in at the local level through Agenda 21. It is easy to overlook local government since people are saturated with too much information in the Internet age. Compounding this is the fact that Agenda 21 is a dull topic, and it's understandable how it has been able to fly mostly under the radar since 1992, slowly working its way into our cities and counties.

Agenda 21, which reportedly means an agenda for the 21st Century, is a United Nations program launched in 1992 for the vague purpose of achieving global "sustainable development." Congress never approved Agenda 21, although Presidents Obama, Clinton and George H.W. Bush have all signed Executive Orders implementing it. The United Nations has mostly bypassed national governments, using Agenda 21's International Council of Local Environmental Initiatives (ICLEI) to make agreements directly with local governments. ICLEI's United States presence has grown to include agreements with over 600 cities, towns and counties here, which are now copying the land use plans prescribed in Agenda 21.

Some conservatives are trying to attract attention to Agenda 21 by labeling it a secret conspiracy to create a one-world government. While that will wake some people up, it will turn others off. It does not matter whether it is a conspiracy or not. There are people on the left side of the political spectrum who may even believe they have good intentions...working together to spread their vision for society worldwide. Whether they meet in dark rooms or openly in public meetings is irrelevant; they are having great success convincing local governments in the United States to adopt their socialist and extreme environmentalist programs under the guise of feel-good buzz words. Left wing billionaire George Soros' Open Society has provided $2,147,415 to ICLEI. Van Jones' (remember him...Obama's original selection for Green czar) Green for All and the Tides Foundations' Apollo Alliance are also reportedly ICLEI contributors.

Agenda 21 ostensibly seeks to promote "sustainability" (the latest revisionist word for "environmentalism," since Americans have learned too many negative things about environmentalism). "Sustainability" is an amorphous concept that can be interpreted to an extreme degree that would regulate and restrict many parts of our lives. When will the level of carbon emissions be low enough? How much must we reduce our consumption of fossil fuels? Preserving the environment is a dubious science, and what steps are really necessary to protect the environment is anyone's guess.

Agenda 21 promotes European socialist goals that will erode our freedoms and liberties. Most of its vague, lofty sounding phrases cause the average person's eyes to glaze over, making it easier to sneak into our communities. The environmentalist goals include atmospheric protection, combating pollution, protecting fragile environments, and conserving biological diversity. Agenda 21 goes well beyond environmentalism. Other broad goals include combating poverty, changing consumption patterns, promoting health, and reducing private property ownership, single-family homes, private car ownership, and privately owned farms. It seeks to cram people into small livable areas and institute population control. There is a plan for "social justice" that will redistribute wealth.

Once these vague, overly broad goals are adopted, they will be interpreted to allow massive amounts of new, overreaching regulations. Joyce Morrison from Eco-logic Powerhouse says, "Agenda 21 is so broad it will affect the way we live, eat, learn and communicate." Berit Kjos, author of Brave New Schools, warns that Agenda 21 regulations would severely limit water, electricity, and transportation...even deny human access to our most treasured wilderness areas, it would monitor all lands and people. No one would be free from the watchful eye of the new global tracking and information system. Even one of the authors of Agenda 21 has admitted that it calls for specific changes in the activities of all people. These steps are already being enacted little by little at the local levels.

Since the United States is one of the wealthiest countries in the world, and uses more energy than any other country, it stands to lose the most from environmental regulations. The goal of "sustainability," which comes down to using government to heavy-handedly accomplish vague goals of caring for the earth, goes contrary to our free market capitalism. Even more unfair, struggling third world countries and communist countries that cannot financially afford to comply with the onerous environmental regulations will continue their high levels of fossil fuel consumption, and the United States will be forced by United Nations regulators to conserve even more to make up for those countries.

Earlier this month, Obama signed Executive Order 13575, establishing the White House Rural Council as prescribed by Agenda 21. The amount of government Obama has directed to administer this is staggering. Obama committed thousands of federal employees in 25 federal agencies to promote sustainability in rural areas, completely bypassing Congressional approval. Some of these agencies are unrelated to rural areas. The agencies will entice local communities into adopting Agenda 21 programs by providing them millions of dollars in grants. Dr. Ileana Johnson Paugh writing for Canada Free Press analyzed the order and wrote, "it establishes unchecked federal control into rural America in education, food supply, land use, water use, recreation, property, energy, and the lives of a high percentage of the United States' population."

Although Agenda 21 is labeled and promoted as "another" feel-good-necessity to ensure the survival of the global community, it has nothing to do with benefiting mankind... but has everything to do with control.

> "The strongest reason for the people to retain the right to keep and bear arms is, as a last resort, to protect themselves against tyranny in government."
>
> Thomas Jefferson

CHAPTER 20

I have touched on various subjects that, to the average politically unaware American, often bring forth conspiracy remarks punctuated with the, "you gotta be kidding," rolling back of the eyes. Well, get ready for even more insight into those disturbing conspiracy theories, because I will be continuing down that road. While there is a long list of individuals who have been a part of the long-running pursuit of a one-world government, a common denominator has kept them connected to an even larger group of powerful collaborators...other individuals and organized groups with vast sums of money and political clout around the world...reaching back 90 years, but always relentlessly pushing forward.

We know that the first attempt at introducing the idea of a one-world government to the world eventually failed because the United States Senate would not ratify the Versailles Treaty. President Wilson was unable to convince congress or the American people to join the League of Nations.

When Colonel House and Wilson, along with other internationalists, realized that America would not join any scheme for a world government without a change in public opinion...was that perhaps a defining moment... an epiphany?

And interestingly enough...as you already know, the CFR was formed during this period of turmoil in American history.

After World War II and the disbanding of the failed League of Nations, America and the departing members of the League of Nations formed the United Nations. But the original...underlying goal, was still intact...to bring the world together under a world government, a new world order.

So exactly what did House and Wilson's realization, that Americans would never join any scheme for a world government without a change in public opinion, say to them...and "the powers that be?"

I believe the powers that be understood that drawing America into a one-world government (A New World Order) would have to be a long, drawn out process of distractions, propaganda, devaluing collectivism and national identity while promoting individualism, class and ethnic disparities, political correctness, victim mentality, government dependence and unfettered immigration...all coming together to create our current global economic downturn. All the above being orchestrated by an ever-growing progressive culture driven by world powers determined to control the global population under the umbrella of a one-world government.

The "dumbing down" of our education systems, with the injection of progressivism's "socialist" teachings, was crucial in steering the movement forward. "Teaching what to think (indoctrination)...as opposed to critical thinking."

Once the majority of Americans become dependent on the government, and thereby willing to accept their government's propaganda that a one-world government would be in the best interest of the whole...there will be strong resistance from the working class. *Therefore, gun control must be accomplished before any transition can even be considered.*

Our military must be weakened beforehand because under a one-world government, only they will have a standing army supplied by the member nations. Individual nations will only be allowed a small "National Guard" like group to handle internal problems.

When the 2010 census asked people to classify themselves by race, more than 21.7 million...at least 1 in 14, went beyond the standard labels and wrote in such terms as "Arab," "Haitian," "Mexican" and "multiracial."

The unpublished data, the broadest tally to date of such write-in responses, is a sign of a diversifying America that's wrestling with changing notions about race.

The figures show most of the write-in respondents are multiracial Americans or Hispanics, many of whom don't believe they fit within the four government-defined categories of race: white, black, Asian/Pacific Islander or American Indian/Alaska Native. Because Hispanic is defined as an ethnicity and not a race, some 18 million Latinos used the "some other race" category to establish a Hispanic racial identity.

Lopez, the son of a Mexican American father and a German Polish mother, has been checking multiple race boxes since the Census Bureau first offered the option in 2000. In 2010 he checked "some other race" and wrote in "multiracial."

More than 3 million write-ins came from white and black Americans who appear to have found the standard race categories insufficient. They include Arabs, Iranians and Middle Easterners, who don't fully view themselves as "white" and have lobbied in the past to be a separate race category. They also include Italians, Germans, Haitians and Jamaicans who consider ancestry a core part of who they are.

Lopez, who helps run a multiracial awareness group, said he believes the government should provide a wider range of choices on survey forms. "Right now there's a significant segment of the population who feel that the boxes do not adequately represent them," he said.

Over the past decade, the number of people identifying as "some other race" jumped by 3.7 million, or 24 percent. Experts say an increase in the write-in responses could signify limitations to the form and potentially skew government counts of communities' racial makeup.

My point here is that we have...for decades, been increasing our legal immigration quotas...in general numbers, specific skills and a large category of other less specific qualifying criteria. And of course we all know about the situation with our illegal immigration "free-for-all."

I'm just suggesting that we already resemble a snapshot of the global community...are we witnessing *the changing of public opinion* as our populace becomes more and more international in makeup?

Much consternation is spent on inequality of income and related advantages in life. Much of the media has recently been obsessing about Mitt Romney's wealth, whether he pays enough in taxes, and how big are the homes of the Republican presidential hopefuls.

All this is treated by most media producers and reporters as if it were some kind of moral or political imperative... that we must all enjoy equal benefits and burdens, although few will say why that would be a good thing or why it is right to aim for it, considering that inequality is clearly the norm throughout mankind's history.

Isaiah Berlin is supposed to have stated that equality is a virtual axiomatic norm of social-political life...regardless; it is widely embraced by philosophers at top schools everywhere. It made its appearance in political history mainly through the writings of the French philosopher Jean Jacques Rousseau. He summarized the idea very succinctly when he stated, "It is very important to understand that justice has much to do with everyone being treated fairly."

This is not quite how some of the greatest thinkers on the topic of justice (Socrates, Plato and Aristotle) understood the concept. Justice to them was more about treating people as they deserved to be treated, based on how they conducted or failed to conduct themselves.

Yet, as hard as I have tried to locate an argument for the idea that equality is the normal state of affairs, I haven't been able to find one. Even as a matter of moral intuition, a wobbly idea but one favored by many contemporary thinkers in ethics; it doesn't appear to be plausible that everyone ought to be enjoying the same conditions of life and that when they don't, it becomes a political and legal imperative to rearrange things so that they will.

Of course, we have different areas of equality before us, and some do appear to be imperative, such as equal protection of our legal rights. But this is about procedural matters, not about results.

Perhaps just the fact of our humanity alone supports

the equality that egalitarians promote? Yet while people are alike in that all are human, our humanity entails immense and legitimate, diversity and inequality.

Just take a peek around you and confirm the plain fact that inequality is everywhere...in talents, beauty, athletic prowess, luck (good and bad), etc. And there is, of course, the widespread inequality of wealth among us...which appears to annoy so many people. I am not convinced it really does since wealth inequality is all around us, and peace still prevails among most of us. No doubt there are people who are heavily beset with envy, and for them... the Occupy Wall Street mob, all inequality of advantage justifies massive political efforts to even things out.

In life, including human affairs, inequality is routine. What matters is whatever inequality exists...that it not be the results of violence or coercion. We will always have the over-achievers and the under-achievers, but as long as the over-achievers' outcome was acquired peacefully, without force and/or unlawfulness against those who underachieve...then, such is life.

Trying to undo the inequalities merely increases the coercive power of some people...thus introducing the most insidious form of human inequality.

And yes, that one-world government (New World Order) will be a socialist state, and if you think Obama's redistribution plan is bad now, just wait until it becomes a global redistribution system. It will most certainly apply itself to leveling that inequality/fairness playing field.

We're already giving some level of aid/assistance to a large percentage of the world's 194 countries. But the bigger problem here is that corrupt government officials of those countries often siphon much of that money off the top.

In his book, The Road To Serfdom, F. A. Hayek warned of the danger of tyranny that inevitably results from government control of economic decision-making through central planning, and in which he argues that the abandonment of individualism, classical liberalism, and freedom inevitably leads to socialist or fascist oppression and tyranny and the serfdom of the individual. Significantly, he challenged the general view among British academics that fascism was a capitalist reaction against socialism, instead arguing that fascism and socialism had common roots in central economic planning and the power of the state over the individual.

He argues that Western democracies, including the United Kingdom and the United States, have "progressively abandoned that freedom in economic affairs without which personal and political freedom has never existed in the past." Society has mistakenly tried to ensure continuing prosperity by centralized planning, which inevitably leads to totalitarianism. "We have in effect undertaken to dispense with the forces which produced unforeseen results and to replace the impersonal and anonymous mechanism of the market by collective and 'conscious' direction of all social forces to deliberately chosen goals." Socialism, while presented as a means of assuring equality, does so through "restraint and servitude," while "democracy seeks equality in liberty." Because planning is coercive, it is an inferior method of regulation, while the cooperation of a free market is superior "because it is the only method by which our activities can be adjusted to each other without coercive or arbitrary intervention of authority."

Centralized planning is inherently undemocratic, because it requires "that the will of a small minority be imposed upon the people." The power of these minorities to act by taking money or property in pursuit of centralized goals...destroys the Rule of Law and individual freedoms.

Where there is centralized planning, the individual would more than ever become a mere means to be used by the authority in the service of such abstractions as the "social welfare" or for the "good of the community." Even the very poor have more personal freedom in an open society than a centrally planned one. While the last resort of a competitive economy is the bailiff, the ultimate sanction of a planned economy is the hangman. Socialism is a hypocritical system, because its professed humanitarian goals can only be put into practice by brutal methods "of which most socialists disapprove." "Such centralized systems also require effective propaganda, so that the people come to believe that the state's goals are their goals."

Hayek analyzed the roots of Nazism in socialism, and then drew parallels to the thoughts of British leaders:

The increasing veneration for the state, the admiration of power, and of bigness for bigness' sake, the enthusiasm for "organization" of everything (we now call it "planning") and that "inability to leave anything to the simple power of organic growth"...are all scarcely less marked in England now than they were in Germany.

Hayek believed that after World War II, "wisdom in the management of our economic affairs would be even more important than before and that the fate of our civilization will ultimately depend on how we solve the economic problems we shall then face." The only chance to build a decent world is "to improve the general level of wealth" via the activities of free markets. He saw international organization as involving a further threat to individual freedom. He concluded: "The guiding principle that a policy of freedom for the individual is the only truly progressive policy, remains as true today as it was in the nineteenth century."

"When plunder becomes a way of life for a group of men living together in society, they create for themselves...in the course of time, a legal system that authorizes it and a moral code that justifies it."

Frederic Bastiat

CHAPTER 21

In 1911, President William Howard Taft ordered 20,000 troops to patrol the United States/Mexico border in response to the Mexican Revolution.

What a concept...imagine that, America securing its international borders.

In 1916, Mexican raiders led by Pancho Villa attacked Columbus, New Mexico, killing 18 Americans.

I guess that explains things, we've never really had the "determination" to adequately monitor and control our borders. The flow from Mexico and Latin America has continued unabated even as "most" administrations made veiled attempts at stemming the tide...or at least producing temporarily ebbs in the flood.

Barack Obama recently assured El Salvador that the United States would not deport more of the 200,000 Salvadorans residing illegally in the United States. As the election nears, and Obama looks to court Hispanic voters, he also created a new position of "public advocate" for illegal immigrants. The advocate's duties appear to encourage millions to circumvent, rather than follow, current federal laws.

The administration has also said it will focus enforcement only on those who have committed crimes...with the implicit understanding that it is no longer a crime to illegally enter and reside in the United States. It is time that Americans revisit the issue and consider very carefully the morality of entering the United States illegally.

American employers have welcomed illegal aliens as a source of cheap labor. Employers were happy to pass the ensuing social costs on to taxpayers. To summarily deport those who have resided here for 20 years, obeyed the law, worked hard, stayed off public assistance and are now willing to pay a fine, demonstrate English proficiency and pass a citizenship test would be impractical, callous and counterproductive.

Most, however, do not fit these reasonable criterions. More importantly, we forget that the influx of millions of illegal aliens unfairly undercuts the wages of the working American poor, especially in times of high unemployment.

Crossing the border was also hardly a one-time infraction. It was the beginning of serial unethical behavior, as illegal aliens on everyday forms and affidavits were not truthful about their immigration status.

The legal process of immigrating to America was reduced to a free-for-all rush to the border. Millions of applicants abroad wait patiently, if not naively, in line to have their education, skills and capital resources evaluated. They are punished with delay or rejection because they alone follow immigration law.

Billions of dollars in state and federal social services

do not just help provide parity to illegal aliens, but also free them to send back about $50 billion in remittances to their home countries each year. That staggering sum also suggests that Mexico and other Latin American governments, as an element of national policy, quite cynically export human capital to gain United States dollars, rather than make the necessary economic, social and political reforms to keep their citizens at home.

Liberals have turned illegal immigration into an issue of identity and tribal politics. Too many advocates for open borders and amnesty argue about the politics of ethnic solidarity rather than considerations of immigration law. We do not hear much in defense of the occasional Pole, Nigerian or Korean who overstays his tourist visa, but rather equate the circumvention of immigration law almost exclusively with social justice for Latinos.

How reactionary and illiberal that debate has become, when Mexican Americans who object to the undermining of immigration law are slandered as sellouts, while non-Hispanics who do the same are smeared as racists and nativists.

In fact, illegal immigration unfairly warped perceptions of undeniable Hispanic success. If one does not include millions of recently arrived poor Latin American foreign nationals in federal and state surveys, then Hispanic American citizens prove statistically to be assimilating, intermarrying, integrating and finding economic success at rates comparable to many other immigrant groups of the past.

To mean anything, laws must be followed. When illegals choose to ignore them, then the entire structure of jurisprudence crashes as well. If foreigners are free to ignore federal immigration law, then shouldn't citizens be able to pick and choose which statutes they find inconvenient?

Finally, illegal immigration has wrongly been couched in terms of a xenophobic and insensitive exploiter preying on a more noble and defenseless guest. In truth, the United States is the most generous host in the world and never more so than during the present age.

There are now about 40 million foreign-born people residing in the United States, both legal and illegal immigrants. That is both the greatest absolute number and percentage of the population in our nation's history. No other country in the world is more liberal in its legal immigration policies or has been more caring toward new arrivals.

We can argue about the history or the future of illegal immigration, but please spare us the psychodramatic appeals to a higher morality.

In most regards, illegal immigration has proven as immoral as it is unlawful.

America has a long history of unrestrained immigration... legal and illegal, but until recent history this influx of humanity was, for the most part, congenial to our prevailing culture and Christian faith. They arrived here with the intention of becoming Americans and upholding American values.

Today we are experiencing a growing religious culture that is in conflict with our foundational base. It is seeking to usurp our way of life and eventually impose its laws and customs on America. History has proven over and over again that Christianity and Islam do not make for tolerant neighbors.

Jonathon Turley, a law professor at George Washington University, reports on a disturbing case in which a state judge in Pennsylvania threw out an assault case involving a Muslim attacking an atheist for insulting the Prophet Muhammad.

Judge Mark Martin, an Iraq war veteran and a convert to Islam, threw the case out in what appears to be an invocation of Sharia law. The incident occurred at the Mechanicsburg, Pennsylvania, Halloween parade where Ernie Perce, an atheist activist, marched as a zombie Muhammad. Talaag Elbayomy, a Muslim, attacked Perce, and was arrested by police.

Judge Martin threw the case out on the grounds that Elbayomy was obligated to attack Perce because of his culture and religion. Judge Martin stated that the First Amendment of the Constitution does not permit people to provoke other people. He also called Perce, the plaintiff in the case, a "doofus." In effect, Perce was the perpetrator of the assault, in Judge Martin's view, and Elbayomy the innocent. The Sharia law that the Muslim attacker followed trumped the First Amendment.

The Washington Post recently reported on an appeals court decision to maintain an injunction to stop the implementation of an amendment to the Oklahoma state constitution that bans the use of Sharia law in state courts. The excuse the court gave was that there was no documented case of Sharia law being invoked in an American court. Judge Martin would seem to have provided that example, which should provide fodder for the argument as the case goes through the federal courts.

The text of the First Amendment could not be clearer. "Congress shall make no law respecting an establishment of religion, or prohibiting the free exercise thereof." It does not say, "Unless somebody, especially a Muslim, is angered." Indeed Judge Martin specifically decided to respect the establishment of a religion...in this case, Islam.

That Judge Martin should be removed from the bench and severely sanctioned goes without saying. He clearly had no business hearing the case in the first place, since he seems to carry an emotional bias. He also needs to retake a constitutional law course. Otherwise, a real can of worms has been opened up, permitting violence against people exercising free speech.

It should be noted that another atheist, dressed as a Zombie Pope, was marching beside the Zombie Muhammad. No outraged Catholics attacked him.

It seems we're approaching a tipping point on mankind's evolutionary horizon where the survival of the species hinges on creating one large village...rather than the primal, tribal mentality. Well, that's what the "powers that be" are pushing for and our government, along with a large portion of our population have seemingly accepted, in the abstract...the principle of the reality of the coming New World Order.

The Islamic Circle of North America (ICNA) Sharia law campaign: ICNA is a Muslim Brotherhood-connected organization whose stated goal is restoring the Islamic caliphate and imposing Sharia law around the world.

When nations and cultures ignore the early warning signs of the infiltration of radical Islam, they pay a very dear price. The United Kingdom has 85 Sharia courts. France has over 750 "no go zones," Muslim enclaves where even French police don't enter.

I'm sure most of the people in Belgium never believed this

could happen in their country...but Muslim immigrants are currently overwhelming them. And it's not just the number of arriving immigrants...but also the high birth rate of the Muslim culture, which over the years will eventually elevate them to majority status.

The path of least resistance for Americans is to assume this could never happen here. But it's already making its inroads here...as the case about the Pennsylvania man who dressed up as a "zombie Mohammed" demonstrates. First the judge lectured him, calling him insensitive... and then, astonishingly, dismissed the charges against the Muslim attacker.

Perhaps a foreboding glimpse into America's future...?

CHAPTER 22

H istory: "Everything" (yes, everything) we're witnessing today has its roots in our past. The seeds of change were sown before most of us were even conceived. And now, as the old proverb promised..."Our chickens are coming home to roost."

As an "old school" American, I am concerned about the direction America is heading. Our leaders, senators, congressional representatives, United States Supreme Court justices, etc. have made some decisions I find disturbing.

Within the last few years changes have been made to our country that I previously would have thought impossible. First, the idea that "corporations are people" and have the same rights as an individual with regard to political contributions is absurd.

The American political system has always been greatly affected by money, but this decision to allow corporations to contribute unlimited amounts of money to a political campaign will quickly turn our democratic republic into nothing more than an oligarchy where a small number of un-elected people with enormous wealth have virtual control of our government and country.

The other decision that I still have a hard time believing actually happened, was for the federal government to have the power to arrest and indefinitely detain anyone, including American citizens, suspected of terrorist involvement. No trial, no proof, no conviction is required. All that is required is an accusation and a suspicion, and someone/anyone could virtually be locked up and have the key thrown away.

I still have a hard time wrapping my head around that one. No "innocent until proven guilty?" No "right to a trial by a jury of my peers?" No "due process?"

Every American citizen should be very concerned about both of these issues and their larger implications for the direction in which our country is being taken.

In a recent interview with Egyptian television, Supreme Court Justice Ruth Bader Ginsburg insulted the United States Constitution and advised Egypt to look somewhere else when drafting its own constitution. Justice Ginsburg was asked to give insight on this crucial topic for the post-Mubarak government but focused more on liberal human rights, rather than traditional American freedom.

When describing the nature of a constitution, Justice Ginsburg did appropriately recognize the importance of a constitution and the duty of the citizens to defend it. Justice Ginsburg did not, unfortunately, take her own advice. She undermined the insight of its crafters and stated, "I would not look to the United States Constitution if I were drafting a Constitution in the year 2012." Instead, Justice Ginsburg referred to the constitutions of more supposedly progressive countries, like South Africa (the most admired in the world, by progressives), Canada, and the European Convention on Human Rights. She stated, "I can't speak about what the Egyptian experience should be, because I'm operating under a rather old constitution." "She directly refuted the United States Constitution's relevance today."

For a United States Supreme Court Justice, entrusted with the duty to interpret the Constitution, this type of statement is unacceptable. Justice Ginsburg failed to respect the authority of the document that it is her duty to protect. When given the opportunity to promote American liberty abroad, Justice Ginsburg did just the opposite and pointed Egypt in the direction of progressivism and the liberal agenda.

Mathew Staver, Founder and Chairman of Liberty Counsel and Dean of Liberty University School of Law, said, "For a sitting United States Supreme Court Justice to speak derisively about the Constitution she is sworn to uphold is distressing, to say the least. Justice Ginsburg's comments about our Constitution undermine the Supreme Court as an institution dedicated to the rule of law, as well as our founding document."

Consider these words by John Adams, our second president, who also served as chairman of the American Bible Society.

In an address to military leaders he said, "We have no government armed with the power capable of contending with human passions, unbridled by morality and true religion. Our constitution was made only for a moral and religious people. It is wholly inadequate to the government of any other."

The outcry calling for Supreme Court Justice Ruth Bader Ginsburg's immediate resignation, or prosecution, should be nationwide and across the political spectrum.

Ginsburg has betrayed the Constitution she swore to protect, defend and uphold. For her to clearly express her opinion that our Constitution is outdated, and America should look to the constitutions of other countries is outrageous and treasonous.

She is very indicative of how Progressive-Leftists operate. They are collectivists who deceptively infiltrate academic, media and governmental institutions, because if presented honestly, the vast majority would reject their agenda. They revise, redefine, falsely accuse and flat-out lie to incrementally dismantle the nation from within.

Disingenuous words and phrases such as social justice, social equality and fair share are repeated to create envy, societal division and class warfare. Any opposition to their agenda is met with adolescent, libelous smears of racism simply because the sitting president is half black.

Ginsburg, the biased leftist ACLU lawyer, must never hear another Supreme Court case. By her own words she has proven she isn't qualified to judge a case as it stands against the founding document that she finds invalid.

A second term for Barack Obama would allow him to expand his replacement of Republican-appointed majorities with Democratic ones on the nation's appeals courts, the final stop for almost all challenged federal court rulings.

Despite his slow start in nominating judges and Republican delays in Senate confirmations, Obama has still managed to alter the balance of power on four of the nation's 13 circuit courts of appeals. Given a second term, Obama could have the chance to install Democratic majorities on several others.

Fourteen of the 25 appeals court judges nominated by Obama replaced Republican appointees.

The next president, whether it's Obama or a Republican, also has a reasonable shot at transforming the majority on the Supreme Court, because three justices representing the closely divided court's liberal and conservative wings, as well as its center, will turn 80 before the next presidential term ends.

The three justices are Ruth Bader Ginsburg, the leader of the court's liberal wing, conservative Antonin Scalia, and Anthony Kennedy, who leans conservative but on some issues has provided a decisive vote for the liberals.

The next high court opening would cause a titanic confirmation fight if it would allow a Republican president to cement conservative control of the court by replacing Ginsburg or if Obama could give Democratic appointees a working majority for the first time in decades by replacing Scalia or Kennedy.

The prospect of such dramatic change on the Supreme Court, along with the justices' strikingly high-profile election-year docket could heighten the judiciary's importance as an election issue, said Curt Levey, who heads the conservative Committee for Justice. The justices will hear arguments on Obama's health care overhaul in March and Arizona's immigration crackdown in April. The court could soon decide whether to hear a Texas affirmative action case challenging the use of race as a factor in college admissions.

Obama's picks have yet to surprise anyone with their decisions, said Levey, head of the conservative interest group. "So Obama's liberal critics can rest assured that if he's re-elected, his transformation of the appeals courts will make a big difference in the law."

Party labels do not always foretell a case's outcome. During recent challenges to the Obama administration's health care overhaul, Republican appeals court judges in Cincinnati and Washington cast deciding votes upholding the law, while a Democratic appointee in Atlanta voted to strike down the requirement that most people buy health insurance or pay a penalty.

Still, there is wide agreement that Obama picks have sharply altered the Richmond-based 4th United States Circuit Court of Appeals, which had been dominated by conservative Republican appointees. This is important because Supreme Court nominees often come from the 4th United States Circuit Court of Appeals.

Ginsburg is by no means the only "globalist" sitting on the Supreme Court. Since Obama took office, Elena Kagan and Sonia Sotomayor have joined her and Stephen Breyer on the bench. It doesn't take a law student to understand the importance of voting Obama out of the White House in November...it's extremely critical.

In case you didn't already know: A globalist is someone who advocates globalization.

The Urban Dictionary's definition of globalization: In a nutshell, the integration and exchange of ideas and goods globally. Hence, the term globalization. It benefits the middle class...and especially the rich and powerful, but has hurt the poor and powerless.

Globalization is just another word for new world order and/or one world government.

Globalization is not nearly as ominous sounding as the other two (new world order and/or one world government)... it's the same deceptive wordsmith spin used by the Global Warming alarmists when they changed their message to Climate Change, making it sound more presentable to the gullible public.

Globalization: Did Marx foresee the future of capitalistic development?

Capitalism has accomplished wonders far surpassing Egyptian pyramids, Roman aqueducts, and Gothic cathedrals; it has conducted expeditions that put all former exoduses of nations and crusades in the shadows.

Constant revolutionizing of production, uninterrupted disturbance of all social conditions, everlasting uncertainty and agitation distinguish the bourgeois epoch from all earlier ones. All fixed, fast frozen relations, with their train of ancient and venerable prejudices and opinions, are swept away and all new-formed ones become antiquated before they can ossify. All that is solid melts into air, all that is holy is profaned, and man is at last compelled to face with sober senses his real condition of life and his relations with his kind.

The need of a constantly expanding market for its products chases the bourgeoisie over the entire surface of the globe. It must nestle everywhere, settle everywhere, and establish connections everywhere.

The bourgeoisie has, through its exploitation of the world market, given a cosmopolitan character to production and consumption in every country. To the great chagrin of reactionaries, it has drawn from under the feet of industry the national ground on which it stood. All old-established national industries have been destroyed or are daily being destroyed. They are dislodged by new industries, whose introduction becomes a life and death question for all civilized nations, by industries that no longer work up indigenous raw material, but raw material drawn from the remotest zones; industries whose products are consumed, not only at home, but in every quarter of the globe. In place of the old wants, satisfied by the production of the country, we find new wants, requiring for their satisfaction the products of distant lands and climes. In place of the old local and national seclusion and self-sufficiency, we have intercourse in every direction, universal inter-dependence of nations. And as in material, so also in intellectual production. The intellectual creations of individual nations become common property. National one-sidedness and narrow-mindedness become more and more impossible, and from the numerous national and local literatures, there arises a world literature.

The bourgeoisie, by the rapid improvement of all instruments of production, by the immensely facilitated means of communication, draws all, even the most barbarian, nations into civilization. The cheap prices of commodities are the heavy artillery with which it forces the barbarians' intensely obstinate hatred of foreigners to capitulate. It compels all nations, on pain of extinction, to adopt the bourgeois mode of production; it compels them to introduce what it calls civilization into their midst, i.e., to become bourgeois themselves. In one word, it creates a world after its own image.

The bourgeoisie has subjected the country to the rule of the towns. It has created enormous cities, has greatly increased the urban population as compared with the rural, and has thus rescued a considerable part of the population from the idiocy of rural life. Just as it has made the country dependent on the towns, so it has made barbarian and semi-barbarian countries dependent on the civilized ones, nations of peasants on nations of bourgeois, the East on the West.

> "Tyranny is always better organized than Freedom."
>
> Charles Peguy

CHAPTER 23

I n 1933, Germany's parliament building, the Reichstag, was gutted by fire. Chancellor Adolf Hitler, blaming the communists, used the fire as justification for suspending civil liberties.

We must never doubt that a similar ploy is just a fabrication away, and necessity is always the rationale for more government control. As Ronald Reagan said, "Freedom is never more than one generation away from extinction."

Obama's recent warning to the "un-elected" Supreme Court...not to take an unprecedented extraordinary step of overturning a law that was passed by a strong majority of a democratically elected Congress is outrageous on two levels.

First, to suggest that the Supreme Court shouldn't judge a law's constitutionality challenges the Court's whole reason for being. It shows a lack of respect for the fundamental structure of our government. There are three independent branches for a reason, and the president runs only one of them, even though it didn't seem that way when he had Pied Piper-like control over

Congress in his first two years. In case he's forgotten, here's what he promised:

"I do solemnly swear or affirm that I will support and defend the Constitution of the United States against all enemies, foreign and domestic; that I will bear true faith and allegiance to the same; that I take this obligation freely, without any mental reservation or purpose of evasion; and that I will well and faithfully discharge the duties of the office on which I am about to enter. So help me God."

Second, the rank audacity demonstrated in his warning is clearly the kind of behavior we see in dictators. He simply wants absolute power regardless of our Constitution. This should be very disturbing even for those who voted for, or plan to vote, for him. Even the liberal justices on the Court should realize this is an overt attempt to compromise their independence, and is yet a higher-level issue than the case at hand. They must send a clear message that the Court's independence is sacrosanct.

I offer this Quote: "The truth is, that, even with the most secure tenure of office, during good behavior, the danger is not, that the judges will be too firm in resisting public opinion, and in defense of private rights or public liberties; but, that they will be ready to yield themselves to the passions, and politics, and prejudices of the day."

Justice Joseph Story, who served from 1811 to 1845.

Did our professor of constitutional law miss that...is the constitutional scholar scolding Justice Story?

For more than two centuries, the Supreme Court has assumed the authority to review acts of Congress and determine their constitutionality one way or the other.

But a professor of constitutional law would know that. Wouldn't he? So, we must ask, is Obama duplicitous or ignorant?

Maybe Obama thinks Story's views on the Constitution no longer apply.

What did Story say about that? "The instrument was not intended to provide merely for the exigencies of a few years, but was to endure through a long lapse of ages, the events of which were locked up in the inscrutable purposes of Providence."

But our Scholar in Chief probably knew that too, huh?

Of course, he knows exactly what he's doing. He was intentionally attempting to mislead the "general public" when he said that striking down ObamaCare would show an "unprecedented" lack of "judicial restraint." His characterization of the Supreme Court's role was "a purposeful distortion." He's already gearing up his blame-game, hedging ahead of the possibility that the court will strike it down all together or at the very least... toss the mandate that everyone buys in.

One of the highly developed talents of Obama is his ability to say things that are demonstrably false, and make them sound not only plausible...but also inspiring. But watch what he actually does, because there is no correlation or connectivity between his words and his actions.

The Obama administration is currently "as close to a monarchy as there has been since the days of King George III."

Are we no longer "citizens" in the eye of the Obama administration, but in fact, "subjects" to an autocratic

President who has trampled the Constitution, seized power far beyond his office, and imposed "mandates" that differ little from dictatorial commands?

In spite of this...and the facts regarding three years of economic stagnation, a failed trillion-dollar stimulus, consecutive years of trillion-dollar budget deficits, a health care bill being challenged in the Supreme Court and some seriously questionable policy decisions, a recent poll by the Washington Post and ABC television found Obama's approval rating reaching 50 percent and gave him a double-digit lead over the most likely Republican nominee. True, the actual campaign hasn't officially started and his liberal collaborators in the mainstream media conducted this poll, but the writing is on the wall.

As Obama's reelection campaign gears-up to deal with the unenviable task of concocting a favorable spin for his miserable record over the past three years, his own false promises will be his team's biggest challenges to reconcile.

"That's why today, I'm pledging to cut the deficit "we inherited" by half by the end of my first term in office." This categorical pledge occurred exactly three years ago this week, February 23, 2009.

Obama followed that insincere pledge with yet another disingenuous assurance that, "If I don't have this done in three years, then there's going to be a one-term proposition."

Here we are three years later, and Obama's promises have evaporated like the rest of his pompous "hope and change" message. Rather than restore economic vigor as promised, trillions of new dollars in wasteful deficit spending primarily benefited his well-connected supporters such as labor bosses and environmental extremists, and slowed our natural cyclical recovery. His administration promised that his policies would cap unemployment at 8 percent all the way back in October 2009, and be down to near 6 percent today. Instead, we've remained above the 8 percent mark...for the most consecutive months since the government began keeping records in the 1940s.

And as for the deficit, Obama most certainly didn't cut it in half. He multiplied it.

In 2008, the federal deficit stood at a retrospectively mild $455 billion. Obama's deficit projection for 2013 reaches $901 billion...twice as much as the 2008 deficit, not half.

Keep in mind that in 2009, the Obama Administration predicted the 2012 deficit would be just $580 billion, so its 2013 projection is hardly reliable.

Obama apologists ascribe the 2009 deficit to the Bush Administration, but that ignores several facts. Obama presided over two-thirds of that 2009 fiscal year, which included such items as his $800 billion failed "stimulus" spending, his counterproductive "Cash for Clunkers" program and the wasteful omnibus bill that included over 8,500 earmarks despite more false promises to end that practice. Accordingly, it's not as though the 2009 budget was somehow set in stone or beyond any control for the candidate who claimed such omnipotent transformational status.

Moreover, the three consecutive deficits under Obama since 2009 have maintained unprecedented levels, proving that initial year wasn't some sort of anomaly attributable to his all-purpose scapegoat George W. Bush.

Obama also offers the excuse that he simply had no understanding of the magnitude of the last recession, and that his spending somehow prevented another depression.

Those claims are also false. First, during the 2008 campaign, Obama characterized the nation's economy in the most catastrophic terms, such as when he said, "This country and the dream it represents are being tested in a way that we haven't seen in nearly a century." Well, the last recession wasn't as pronounced as the early 1980s recession that Ronald Reagan's pro-growth policies overcame, so if anything Obama was exaggerating the crisis before he was even elected.

During that same 2008 campaign Obama labeled deficit levels of the Bush era "unpatriotic." If Bush deficits ranging between $157 billion and $413 billion (the largest Bush deficit at the time Obama leveled that charge) were "unpatriotic," how might we characterize his deficits? Criminal? Traitorous? Just wondering.

Economic data shows that we were already beginning to recover before Obama even took office, and certainly before any of his policies took effect. By the third quarter of 2009, before Obama had even been in office six months, the recession ended and returned to positive territory.

Thus, the economic "free fall" that Obama now attempts to portray in order to excuse his record is a myth.

There is one promise, however, that the Obama Administration remains on track to keep, one that touches upon a topic leading the headlines in recent weeks. In September 2008, Obama's (soon to be) Secretary of Energy Steven Chu said, *"Somehow we have to figure out how to boost the price of gasoline to the levels in Europe."* Almost four years later, gasoline prices have climbed from $2.00 when he was inaugurated to over $4.00 (in California) today, a record high for the month of February 2012.

Otherwise, however, the litany of Obama's broken promises is long. We cannot change the damage inflicted over the past three years, but those promises provide the clearest standard by which Americans can evaluate his request for four more years.

I fear the president will win re-election, not because of any successes, but because he has the backing of the unions, the minority community, including a near-unanimous African American voting bloc, and an ever-increasing number of Americans receiving government assistance. The truth is that the unions are cutting their own throats; minorities, especially African Americans, are being hurt by the president's policies; and, sooner or later the government won't be able to pay for the promises being made. It doesn't matter because perception is more persuasive than cold, hard facts.

Perception is formed in large part by the media and to a lesser extent by the education and entertainment industries. These institutions, and again, most importantly, the media, are solidly behind Obama. Liberals claim that liberal media bias is a myth and then rail about "Faux News" and talk radio.

Studies estimate that this slant in media coverage gives liberal candidates an advantage of 8 to 10 percent in national elections. Tens of billions of dollars are spent on advertising every year to sway people toward one product or another because advertising works. This is the most reasonable explanation available to clarify how Obama can still reach a 50 percent approval rating in spite of ruinous policies and broken promises.

Compare the media coverage of the Tea Party with that of the Occupy Movement. The Tea Party was demonized for opposing raising the debt limit and earlier was labeled racist for alleged slurs against black congressmen that were never proven. The Occupy Movement has behaved in absolutely reprehensible ways time after time, resulting in millions of dollars in damage, while their documented anti-Semitic slurs were largely ignored.

The result was that in an October opinion poll, 65 percent of respondents said the Tea Party's influence was negative, while 23 percent said they had a negative opinion of the Occupy Movement.

Contrast the media coverage of Herman Cain's alleged sexual misdeeds with those of President Clinton. When Cain's first anonymous accuser came forward the media went wild. After Gloria Allred's accuser came forward, one reporter asked Mr. Cain if he would be willing to take a lie detector test. The media in the 1990s showed no equal interest in President Clinton's alleged affairs and allegations of an actual rape. Cain quit the presidential race, and Clinton has become a Democratic icon.

I hope I'm wrong, but the deck is definitely stacked against whomever the Republicans nominate.

I would say that in any election, conservatives should vote for the most electable conservative. But the codicil might be, unless the nomination or election of a particular conservative would mean a net long-term subtraction from conservatism's strength.

The current front-runners might not cause such subtraction, as they are conservatives...although of strikingly different stripes. But there doesn't seem to be an electable one in the pack. No one has demonstrated, or seems likely to develop, an aptitude for energizing a national coalition that translates into 270 electoral votes.

Whoever is nominated, conservatives should vote for him. But suppose the accumulation of evidence eventually suggests that the nomination of "whoever" would subtract from the long-term project of making conservatism intellectually coherent and politically palatable. If so, there would come a point when, taking stock of reality, conservatives turn their energies to a goal more attainable than, and not much less important than, electing their nominee. That goal would be retaining control of the House and winning control of the Senate.

Several possible Supreme Court nominations and the staffing of the regulatory state are among the important reasons conservatives should try to elect whomever the GOP nominates. But conservatives this year should have as their primary goal, to make sure Republicans wield all the gavels in Congress in 2013.

If Republicans can do that, their committee majorities will serve as fine-mesh filters, removing Obama's initiatives from the stream of legislation.

This may be a dubious achievement, but it certainly enlarges the power of a congressional party to play defense against a president.

Such a restoration would mean that a re-elected Obama...a lame duck at noon next January 20...would have a substantially reduced capacity to do more harm.

From Louisiana's Governor Bobby Jindal to Wisconsin's Representative Paul Ryan, Republicans have a rising generation of potential 2016 candidates. This does not mean conservatives should be indifferent to the fate of this year's nominee, and it is perhaps premature to despair over who will eventually emerge as our nominee and his political aptitude.

This November American voters will face a stark choice. They can opt to re-elect a president who is committed to increasing the role of their government...European-style, with higher taxes and stagnating economic growth...or, they can follow a path consistent with our historic values of liberty, innovation, and free enterprise. A battle for the future of America is under way, and the winner has yet to be determined...

Researchers are challenging the assumption that most citizens can recognize the best political candidate when they see him.

Research has revealed an unfortunate aspect of the human psyche that would seem to disprove this notion, and implies instead that democratic elections produce mediocre leadership and policies.

Incompetent people are incapable to judge the competence of others, or even the quality of their ideas. For example, if voters lack expertise on tax reform, how can they identify a candidate who knows what he is talking about when it comes to tax reform? They simply lack the mental tools to make such judgments.

This may explain how Americans chose a community activist devoid of any executive skills to be the nation's chief executive.

Who would deem such a man competent to hold the office of the world's most powerful country? Voters of similar... or less, intellectual competence, that's who...Dumb and Dumber.

The researchers concluded that it won't matter how

much information or how many facts voters are given. The inherent inability of many of them to make sense of the data means arriving at a smart conclusion will be a long shot.

"We always want the best man to win an election, but unfortunately he never runs." Mused folksy political sage Will Rogers.

There was a day in the United States of America when we allowed only the best and brightest, or at least that's what they insisted they were, to vote and to hold office. But within short years of 1776, suffrage broadened throughout the land. Bars to holding office were lowered. Larger segments of the population beyond property-owning white guys were permitted the franchise. Nevertheless, allowing nearly any sentient human being to vote hasn't helped much, if at all.

It seems a large percentage of Americans regard the four remaining Republican presidential candidates unfavorably, according to a Washington Post/ABC News poll last week. That, in the words of a Post reporter, is a sobering reminder for the party that the extended primary season has damaged the brand.

It appears that the more those perhaps not-so-bright voters are exposed to those apparently less-than-impressive candidates, the less they like them.

To sum up, candidates who have failed to inspire even the most committed voters, who are more likely to have convictions to help them sort wheat from chaff, now are facing increasing pressure to appeal to the muddled middle, who apparently have fewer convictions and less ability to discern.

Of those the Post identifies as "independent voters,"

no Republican candidate last week had higher than a 38-percent favorable rating, and that was Ron Paul, whose chances of winning the nomination are about as good as Rush Limbaugh's. The GOP frontrunner, former Massachusetts governor Mitt Romney, trailed with a dismal 32 percent favorable score, and that was 16 points lower than the 48 percent of independents who viewed Romney unfavorably.

Voters may not be the best judges of competence in presidential candidates, and virtually no Republican candidate for president appears acceptable to "independent" voters, who probably will decide the outcome.

There's another dimension to this perplexing problem. The Wall Street Journal reported that a poll on the ObamaCare mandate had 53 percent support and 33 percent opposed. But when people were asked about applying the mandate to religiously affiliated hospitals and colleges with the insurer paying the cost, support dropped sharply to 38 percent. When the morning-after pill was specifically mentioned concerning Catholic institutions, support for the mandate dropped further, to 34 percent.

In other words, one could deduce that the less a voter knows about the ObamaCare mandate, the more likely they are to support it.

The devil, they say, is in the details. If exposure brings more awareness of issues, it certainly must have the same effect on candidates, who are nothing if not bundles of issues. Gratuitous sound bites and glamour photos give a yearlong campaign, a lot of up-close-and-personal inspections.

In other words, the less you know about candidates,

the more likely you are to support them. And of course the media's deliberate lack of gathering background information...their epic failure in vetting Obama is what allowed him to find his way into the highest office in the land.

It really shouldn't require much smarts to make good choices. Weighing candidates against the golden standard of their humility and devotion to mercy and justice factors, such as good vs. evil, right vs. wrong, freedom vs. slavery. But it does however require a measure of wisdom.

Wisdom recognizes that it is not charity to forcibly take from one in order to give to another, even under color of authority. Robin Hood was not charitable. He was a thief. It is not justice to infringe on one person's God-given rights to property, religion and speech in order to provide benefits to another. Our nation's principles stem from 1776, not 2008.

So, the question as we proceed down the stretch in the primary and then the general election is whether voters will be wise enough, even if they aren't smart enough, and then whether any candidate can emerge as worthy enough, rising out of the muck of endless recriminations, perhaps at a brokered convention.

We should know by now that it's useless to attempt to reason an individual out of something he or she was never reasoned into.

I hope I'm wrong, but I would suggest that if he's given another four years...it would not be out of the realm of possibilities that we would not see another election in 2016.

Footnote on Obama's re-election campaign slogan, "Forward."

We certainly know his first campaign slogan was vague and without substance...it was a mirage, but it delivered what it promised...nothing tangible. The new slogan sounds like another smoke and mirrors shell game, but if we look backward instead of "Forward"...we see that it does in fact have history and substance. The word has a long and rich association with European Marxism.

Many Communist and radical publications and entities throughout the 19th and 20th centuries had the name "Forward" or its foreign cognates.

Wikipedia has an entire section called "Forward":

The online encyclopedia explains that the name "Forward" carries a special meaning in socialist political terminology. It has frequently been used as a name for socialist, communist and other left-wing newspapers and publications.

The slogan "Forward!" reflected the conviction of European Marxists and radicals that their movements replicated the march of history, which would move them forward... past capitalism and into socialism and communism.

The Obama campaign released its new campaign slogan Monday in a 7-minute video. The title card simply has the word "Forward" with the 'O' having the familiar Obama logo from 2008. It will be played at rallies this weekend marking the Obama re-election campaign's official beginning.

There have been at least two radical-left publications named 'Vorwaerts' (the German word for "Forward"). One was the daily newspaper of the Social Democratic Party of Germany whose writers included Friedrich Engels and Leon Trotsky. It still publishes as the organ of Germany's Social Democratic Party, though that party has changed considerably since World War II. Another was the 1844 biweekly reader of the Communist League. Karl Marx, Friedrich Engels and Mikhail Bakunin are among the names associated with that publication.

Vladimir Lenin founded the publication 'Vpered' (the Russian word for "Forward") in 1905. Soviet propaganda filmmaker Dziga Vertov made a documentary whose title is sometimes translated as "Forward, Soviet."

Conservative critics of the Obama administration have noted numerous ties to radicalism and socialists throughout Obama's history, from his first political campaign being launched from the living room of two former Weather Underground members, to appointing Van Jones (a self-described communist) as green jobs czar.

> "The beginning of wisdom is the fear of the Lord. The next and most urgent counsel is to take stock of reality."
>
> William F. Buckley

CHAPTER 24

It now appears very probable that Mitt Romney will be Obama's challenger in the upcoming November election. It's also very apparent that this election will provide the voting population with two very different arguments: "Fairness vs. Freedom."

These are the same ancient arguments that once pitted the statist visions of John Maynard Keynes against the individualism of Friedrich Hayek, and the tragic admission that we cannot be truly free if we are "forced to be roughly equal" versus the idealism that if we are all roughly equal then we are truly free.

In blunter terms, Romney's message is this: If you have the money to drive a nice Kia, what do you care if a sleek Mercedes whizzes by? Obama's answer, in contrast, is that you should care, because the guy in the Mercedes probably took something from you. Can we say, "Victimology?"

The election will hinge upon how many people who can't afford a Kia now believe that they might be able to under Romney...and who could care less about the other guy in the Mercedes.

"A society that puts equality ahead of freedom will end up with neither equality nor freedom. A society that puts freedom first will, as a happy byproduct, end up with both greater freedom and greater equality." Milton Friedman

So with that said, I will use this chapter to elaborate on a number of ongoing...and very troubling accusations, innuendoes and conspirator theories that have plagued this administration from day one.

Denialism is the culture of denying an established fact, when a person or group refuses to believe or accept a theory, law, fact or evidence of a well-established discipline in an authoritative way. Usually this is despite overwhelming evidence, and usually for motives of convenience. Because of these motives, denialism is often subject to and powered by confirmation bias.

In scientific denialism, the denialist can deny a cause (carbon dioxide does not cause global warming), an effect (global warming does not occur), the association between the two (the earth is warming, but not because of carbon dioxide), the temporal relationship (carbon dioxide concentrations are increased because the earth is warming) or the isolation of the cause-and-effect relationship (other factors than greenhouse gases cause the earth to warm). Often denialists will practice minimization (the earth is warming, but it's not harmful) and will use misplaced skepticism in the veneer of being a scientist when it is unwarranted.

Denialism can also fill a deep psychological need, as in the case of answering the question as to why one's child has autism, where in reality...there is no easy answer.

But most denialist rhetoric is focused at the layperson and not the expert, and usually paints a contrast between two positions rather than being about one point-of-view. First, they skillfully invoke values that are shared by the scientific community and the American public alike, like free speech, skeptical inquiry, and the revolutionary force of new ideas against a repressive orthodoxy. It is difficult to argue against someone who invokes these values without seeming unscientific or un-American.

The mainstream media should be called out for its deliberate neglect of the largest scandal in modern American history. Maricopa County, Arizona Sheriff Joe Arpaio released credible forensic evidence that Barack Obama, "presumed" President of the United States, presented to the world a forged Birth Certificate on April 27th, 2011.

In the summer of 2008, the presidential primary season was winding down, and America could not help but note the fervor a significant number of media personalities expressed while supporting the candidacy of Barack Obama. Indeed, it was collectively decided within the liberal media, that Obama's associations with racist pastors and violent domestic terrorists was to be suppressed.

The exposure of the "Journalist" email scandal in 2010 made this glaringly clear: Stories like Obama's ties to Reverend Jeremiah Wright Jr. of the Trinity United Church, and more relevant, to Bill Ayers and his radical past in the Weather Underground Organization were to remain largely un-reported and uninvestigated. Any realistic investigation into Barack Obama's background was to be minimized, inquiries eventually mocked, and investigators labeled racists.

These tactics have isolated honest media who could and should have reported on these and other important stories yet have inexplicably remained silent. Now we know why.

Since then, the scandal has only expanded. Retired United States Postal Service worker, Allen Hulton, has recently come forward with compelling testimony given under oath, which leads to only one conclusion: Barack Obama attended College in the United States as a Foreign Student.

Hulton recently signed a sworn affidavit for the Maricopa County, Arizona Cold Case Posse convened by Sheriff Joe Arpaio, attesting under oath, to conversations with Mary Ayers, the mother of Bill Ayers. He made his testimony public in a three hour long taped interview on March 19th, 2012. Mr. Hulton, by signing an affidavit has subjected himself to laws regarding perjury, not something to be taken lightly as telling the truth is now... for him, a requirement of law.

His testimony states that Mary and Tom Ayers (parents of Bill "I don't regret setting bombs" Ayers) were sponsoring Barack Obama as a foreign student, and financially supporting his education.

Bill Ayers of dubious "Weatherman" fame, was not just "a guy who lives in my neighborhood," as then candidate Obama brushed aside in a televised DNC Debate in the summer of 2008. As Hillary Clinton revealed then, Obama served in a paid position on the Woods Foundation with Bill Ayers and the two were involved in several projects dispersing millions of dollars over several years.

Realistically, the Ayers family could be said to have adopted Barack Obama, as a kindred Marxist spirit, and treated him to one of the finest educations possible.

There is little doubt Obama has been less than honest

with regard to the Ayers family and their significance in his life. As disingenuous as this is, it is by no means the most important revelation.

If correct, and Obama was introduced to Hulton as a Foreign Student, this means Barack Hussein Obama would have been using a Foreign Passport to get and prove his foreign student status for entrance into Occidental College, Columbia, and later Harvard Universities. Because Hulton has signed an affidavit, this cannot be disregarded as mere hearsay; it is instead evidentiary in nature.

The significance of this development may not be immediately apparent until one recognizes American law regarding citizenship status. Citizenship laws as expressed in Title 8 of the United States Code (8 USC 1481) states the use of a Foreign Passport constitutes adult recognition of relinquishment of American Citizenship.

> ➤ A person who is a national of the United States whether by birth or naturalization, shall lose his nationality by voluntarily performing any of the following acts with the intention of relinquishing United States nationality.

> ➤ Obtaining naturalization in a foreign state upon his own application or upon an application filed by a duly authorized agent, after having attained the age of eighteen years (8 USC 1481).

Using a foreign passport in order to obtain status as a foreign student is precisely that, proof of naturalization in a foreign state.

Obama Sr. was born just outside Kendu Bay, Kenya Colony which, at the time...was a colony of the British Empire. His Certificate of Live Birth is consistent with his commonly reported birth date June 18, 1936. However, about a dozen documents, including an alien registration card with fingerprints and immigration arrival-departure card that presumably accompanied his passport...show a birth date of June 18, 1934. Interesting...like father like son.

While attending a Russian language class at the University of Hawaii, Ann Dunham met Obama Sr., the school's first African student. At the age of 23, Obama Sr. had come to Hawaii to pursue his education, leaving behind a pregnant wife and infant son in his hometown of Nyang'oma Kogelo, in Kenya. Dunham and Obama Sr. were married on the Hawaiian island of Maui on February 2, 1961, despite parental opposition from both families. Dunham was three months pregnant. Obama Sr. eventually informed Dunham about his "other" marriage in Kenya but claimed he was divorced. Years later, she would discover this was false. Obama Sr.'s first wife, Kezia, later said she had granted her consent for him to take/marry a second wife, in keeping with Luo customs.

On August 4, 1961, at the age of 18, Dunham gave birth to her first child, Barack Obama II.

Dunham filed for divorce in January 1964, which Obama Sr. did not contest.

Obama Sr. returned to his native Kenya (formally Kenya Colony) in August 1964 and was killed in a car accident, or possibly murdered in 1982.

Dunham later met Lolo Soetoro, a Javanese surveyor who had come to Honolulu to study geography at the University of Hawaii. In 1965, Soetoro and Dunham were married in Hawaii, and in 1966, Soetoro returned to Indonesia. After her graduation in 1967, Dunham and her six-year-old son moved to Jakarta, Indonesia, to rejoin her husband.

As a child, Barack Obama became an Indonesian Citizen when his stepfather Lolo Soetoro adopted him. Young Barack by law needed the Indonesian Citizenship in order to attend school, and his adoption provided that.

In his defense, Obama supporters have claimed for years if the president had lost his American Citizenship as a child, he did not in fact lose it because the actions of a parent cannot permanently remove a child's American natural born citizenship status. This fallacious argument once had some validity within the confusing morass that is American Citizenship law, the nature of which is a challenge for immigration attorneys even today.

However, Hulton's story and sworn affidavit would confirm that Barack Obama renounced what American citizenship status he had as an adult over the age of 18, by attending college as a foreign student using a foreign passport.

This would explain the president's refusal to release his college records. These records will easily prove or disprove his status as a Foreign Student. This is the importance of United States Postal worker, Allen Hulton's testimony. Unless Obama formally renounced that foreign citizenship, there is the distinct possibility he is not an American Citizen, let alone a Natural Born Citizen.

In reality, due to his fathers British heritage, Mr. Obama was never a Natural Born Citizen to begin with, and admitted precisely that on his "Fight the Smears" website, stating that he was born under the British Nationality Act of 1948.

The British Empire established the East Africa Protectorate

in 1895, known from 1920 as the Kenya Colony. The independent Republic of Kenya was founded in December 1963.

Equally unreported by the United States media is that of the Selective Service Card which registered Barack Obama for the Draft in 1980. Sheriff Arpaio's Cold Case Posse released information on March 1, 2012, that this document is also "highly suspicious" of being a forgery, along with Obama's "Long Form Birth Certificate" which was released by the president in the White House press room on April 27, 2011.

One of the few media outlets reporting fully on the Cold Case Posse is the Tea Party Tribune of Arizona. On March 21, the Tribune reported that Sheriff Arpaio had asked the Selective Service headquarters in Virginia for the original card itself in an effort to determine its authenticity within the Selective Service System. According to the Tribune, Sheriff Arpaio expressed his confidence that the agency would investigate the matter. This remains to be seen.

Has the wider American media addressed any of this in context? It may be the largest scandal in American history, certainly the most significant constitutional crisis the nation has faced since the end of the Civil War.

The First Amendment will not prevent a few thugs funded by a private citizen or corporation from paying strategic individuals personal visits though, will it? Now we know why the remaining honest media has remained suspiciously silent.

Rumors of censorship of the American press have circulated at various times over the last several years. It seemed impossible that such credible and realistic questions, about Obama, still remain un-addressed by the mainstream media. Indeed, the media in general is very aware of these questions, however they cannot ask them, let alone report on them. Just one example is Media Matters, funded by the George Soros Foundation, which has repeatedly and openly threatened Talk Radio hosts like Rush Limbaugh and his advertisers. Many have given in to the threats merely to stay in business.

A telephone interview March 22nd with Cold Case Posse Lead investigator Mike Zullo revealed the Posse had received "highly credible" information from three separate sources detailing information regarding a nationally syndicated Conservative Talk Radio show. This major, very well known host was forced to utilize a fill-in personality the day the script called for a discussion of Barack Obama's persistent and unanswered questions regarding his citizenship status.

The executive producers of the national show pulled the script 3 hours before airtime, literally leaving the host with no script whatsoever. To have a draft tossed just hours before airing is simply not done without explanation or substitution.

Lead Investigator Zullo revealed in this conversation that several individuals have come forth to provide testimony; the identity of these witnesses is being withheld for their protection. They identify producers, reporters, television and radio personalities who have been told specifically by intimidating individuals who state clearly, they are not going to report on this story. These witnesses have been told, "If you breathe a word about this on the air, we will make certain you never work in this business again," said Investigator Zullo. Apparently those making the threats have the power to carry through on them.

There are a few however with the courage to speak out and report on this story. Talk radio show host Rodger

Hedgecock recently had Sheriff Joe Arpaio on his show. "This is probably the biggest censorship blackout in the history of the United States, and it's because it has to do with the White House...the President," said Arpaio. How can the American media possibly pass up a story so huge, and so important...fraud committed by a sitting president? Simple, it has quite basically been threatened into silence, and law enforcement is now well aware of it.

Witnesses have given testimony, but have done so under the very strictest of confidentiality agreements. Collectively they are afraid of losing their jobs, or of their employees being further threatened. Sheriff Arpaio and the Cold Case Posse have the information directly from witnesses who have specific knowledge of the threats, and there are a significant number of informants. Whoever is making these threats has the power to make those threats happen. It is being taken so seriously that no major media outlet has dared to break the silence.

When asked if this was thuggery, Sheriff Arpaio's reply came without hesitation, "That's exactly what it is."

During our investigation, we were told that media had been threatened with FTC investigations and commentators threatened with their jobs. These are the auspices of the federal government with the resources of a powerful nation backing them. The justifications for using such power are almost unlimited.

These federal agencies can yank broadcasting licenses, or take a variety of other actions that have the effect of making it impossible to do business let alone broadcast. It's a brutal quid pro quo; don't breathe a word on Barack Obama's citizenship issues or constitutional qualifications for the office he has usurped, and we will let you stay in business.

To be brutally clear, the power and backing of the United States Federal Government is being used to silence the press about Barack Obama. Either outright or through coercion, the media is complicit in covering up the fraud crimes of Barack Obama and his unconstitutional government. These patterns are clear and unmistakable.

Nine State Attorney Generals who have taken the unprecedented step of listing the continuing crimes of the Obama Administration with the clear intent to prosecute, which has also received little media attention.

Update 3-29-2012:

Richard S. Flahavan, associate Director of Public & Intergovernmental Affairs wrote to Maricopa County Sheriff Joe Arpaio, stating: "This Agency has no evidence that President Obama's 1980 registration is not authentic, however, if you have any credible evidence to the contrary and believe that a Federal crime has been committed, we suggest that it be turned over immediately to the Federal Bureau of Investigation to pursue."

Given that the FBI is under the office of United States Attorney General Eric Holder, it seems very unlikely that any Federal investigation would lead anywhere other than to a dead-end.

CHAPTER 25

"From Mesaba to Titanic: In latitude 42° N to 41° 25', longitude 49° W to longitude 50° 30' W, saw much heavy pack ice and great number large icebergs, also field ice, weather good, clear."

One hundred years ago this week, that heavy ice admonition was one of several transmitted but unheeded by the R.M.S. Titanic following her departure from Southampton, England. She actually received six warnings on April 11, five more on April 12, three on April 13 and seven on April 14 before her fateful collision, which occurred just two hours after the Mesaba's final alert.

The enormous vessel hubristically labeled "unsinkable" couldn't even survive her maiden voyage, which helps explain her enduring, ghastly legacy beyond her survivors' lifetimes. Three years after the Titanic tragedy, nearly as many passengers lost their lives when German U-boats sank the R.M.S. Lusitania, but Titanic's mythology proved far more poignant.

Today, across the Atlantic Ocean that serves as the Titanic's watery tomb, we behold the dysfunction of debt-ridden Greece and Europe more broadly. We scoff at their increasingly chaotic state, which its leaders and citizens should have expected after decades of unsustainable welfare statism. This week, however, the Senate Budget Committee noted that the $15.1 trillion United States debt actually exceeds the combined $12.7 trillion debt of the Euro Zone and United Kingdom. Because our relative populations are roughly equal, our debt exceeds theirs on a per capita basis as well.

Congressman Ryan observes that, "This coming debt crisis is the most predictable crisis we've ever had in this country." In other words, we have seen the Greek iceberg.

In fact, the Treasury Department announced this month that the federal government spent $369 billion during the month of March, more than any month in American history. It also announced a one-month budget deficit of $198 billion, which is also an all-time record for the month of March.

Unlike Titanic Captain Edward Smith, Captain Obama can see the oncoming catastrophe perfectly well.

Course correction...no, full speed ahead.

Medicare also proceeds toward insolvency, but Obama merely demonizes anyone who offers constructive proposals to save it.

Course correction...no, full speed ahead.

And there's ObamaCare. Two years ago, the Obama Administration, Harry Reid's Senate, Nancy Pelosi's House and many of the healthcare industry's most powerful lobbies colluded on that monstrosity. They did so under the assumption that the unconstitutional individual mandate would provide fiscal sustainability by imposing involuntary commercial activity upon every single living American. They didn't even bother to insert a severance clause, whether intentionally or negligently. Following Supreme Court oral argument on the matter, however, they suddenly recognize the looming catastrophe of costly new entitlements without the offsetting new customer base. That was an entirely foreseeable prospect.

But ignore that iceberg as well...full speed ahead. His only course correction was to preemptively and falsely demonize the Supreme Court as a rogue body that would commit the "unprecedented" act of overturning a law imposed by a "strong majority."

The saddest tragedy of the Titanic is that it was avoidable. Unfortunately, the warnings it received remained unheeded.

The stunning arrogance of both men boggles the mind, but their drivers were vastly different. Captain Edward Smith's mistake wasn't so much about personal arrogance but rather his false belief that the Titanic was invincible and indeed, unsinkable. But on the other hand, Captain Obama has seen the icebergs and unlike the Titanic's invincibility, he knows America is vulnerable...and if the necessary course corrections aren't addressed, America... as we've known it, could cease to exist.

One hundred years later, the question is whether we will act to avert the quickly approaching, metaphorical icebergs. Obama doesn't appear too interested in "righting his listing ship of fools," but ultimately it's not his decision whether he'll remain captain.

Years from now, historians may regard the 2008 election of Obama as an inscrutable and disturbing phenomenon, a baffling breed of mass hysteria akin perhaps to the witch craze of the Middle Ages. How, they will wonder, did a man so devoid of professional accomplishment beguile so many into thinking he could manage the world's largest economy, direct the world's most powerful military, and execute the world's most consequential job?

Imagine a future historian examining Obama's pre-presidential life: Ushered into and through the Ivy League despite unremarkable grades and test scores along the way; a cushy non-job as a "community organizer"; a brief career as a state legislator devoid of legislative achievement and finally...an unaccomplished single term in the United States Senate, the entirety of which was devoted to his presidential ambitions. He left no academic legacy in academia, authoring no signature legislation as a legislator.

And then there is the matter of his troubling associations with the white-hating, America-loathing preacher who for decades served as Obama's "spiritual mentor," and a real-life, actual terrorist who served as Obama's colleague and political sponsor. It is easy to imagine a future historian looking at it all and asking, "How on Earth" was such a man elected president?

To be sure, no white candidate who had close associations with an outspoken hater of America like Jeremiah Wright and an unrepentant terrorist like Bill Ayers, would have lasted a single day. But because Obama was black and therefore entitled, in the eyes of liberaldom, to have hung out with protesters against various American injustices, even if they were a bit extreme...he was given a pass.

I think a subliminal form of affirmative action drove the Obama phenomenon. Not in the legal sense, but certainly in the motivating sentiment behind all affirmative action laws and regulations, which are designed primarily to make white people, and especially white liberals, feel good about themselves.

Unfortunately, minorities often suffer so that whites can pat themselves on the back. Liberals routinely admit minorities to schools for which they are not qualified, yet take no responsibility for the inevitable poor performance and high drop-out rates which follow. Liberals don't care if these minority students fail; liberals aren't around to witness the emotional devastation and deflated self-esteem resulting from the racist policy that is affirmative action.

Holding someone to a separate standard merely because of the color of his skin...that's affirmative action in a nutshell, and if that isn't racism, then nothing is.

All his life, every step of the way, Obama was told he was good enough for the next step, in spite of ample evidence to the contrary. What could this breed if not the sort of empty narcissism on display every time Obama speaks?

I'm sure we all remember his series of briefings and the NBC interview in the Situation (War) Room designed to highlight the "gutsy call" he made in approving the bin Laden mission. "I said that I'd go after bin Laden if we had a clear shot at him, and I did," Obama said. But what he didn't say was that he only signed-off on the operation after prolonged urging from the military and defense hierarchy. Of course once the Seals performed their task so effectively...and he couldn't be blamed for a failed attempt, or worse yet...the loss of military personnel; he quickly took full responsibility and credit.

Obama is so obsessed with getting rave reviews that he can't overcome the urge to give himself rave reviews. It's even more awkward when you brag about yourself and the people who really did the deed are still around to hear you. His absurd braggadocio is turning one of the few successes to occur under his leadership into a political liability.

Ryan Zinke, a former Commander in the United States Navy who spent 23 years as a SEAL and led a SEAL Team 6 assault unit, said: "The decision was a no brainer." Both serving and former United States Navy SEALs have taken exception to Obama taking credit for the killing of Osama bin Laden. The elite military force also accused him of using the Special Forces' operation as "ammunition" for his re-election campaign.

It's hard to imagine Lincoln or Eisenhower claiming such credit for the heroic actions of others. That is not to say that great leaders, including presidents, have not placed themselves at the center of great events. But generally it has been to accept responsibility for failure. Yeah, that's not easy to imagine...the self-proclaimed Mr. Hope admitting failure. We know he wouldn't because he hasn't, despite having failed repeatedly for nearly four years.

If anything is obvious about the Orator in Chief, it is how highly he thinks of himself. The "H" for his middle name doesn't stand for "Humility."

I must confess that I was unreceptive from the beginning... not just because of his shallowness but because there was an air of haughtiness in his demeanor that was unsettling. His posture and his body language were louder than his empty words.

The fact that Obama is totally incognito with zero accomplishments makes this inexplicable infatuation alarming. Obama is not an ordinary man, but he is not a genius either...in fact, he is quite ignorant on most important subjects.

I'm certainly not an expert on the subject, but Obama appears to be a narcissist. Narcissists project a grandiose but false image of themselves. Jim Jones, the charismatic leader of People's Temple, the man who led over 900 of his followers to cheerfully commit mass suicide and even murder their own children was also a narcissist. David Koresh, Charles Manson, Joseph Koni, Shoko Asahara, Joseph Stalin, Saddam Hussein, Mao Tsi Tung, Kim Jong IL and Adolph Hitler are a few examples of narcissists of our time. All these men had a tremendous influence over their fanciers. They created a personality cult around themselves and with their blazing speeches elevated their admirers, filled their hearts with enthusiasm and instilled in their minds a new zest for life. They gave them hope! They promised them the moon, but alas, invariably they brought them to their doom. When you are a victim of a cult of personality, you don't know it until it is too late.

One must never underestimate the manipulative genius of pathological narcissists. They project such an imposing personality that it overwhelms those around them. Charmed by the charisma of the narcissist, people become like clay in his hands. They cheerfully do his bidding and delight to be at his service. The narcissist shapes the world around himself and reduces others to his own inverted image. He creates a cult of personality.

His admirers become his co-dependents. Narcissists have no interest in things that do not help them to reach their personal objective. They are focused on one thing alone and that is power. All other issues are meaningless to them and they do not want to waste their precious time on trivialities. Anything that does not help them is beneath them and does not deserve their attention. That's why when he was in the Senate he more often than not, voted "present." It was a safe vote and no one could criticize him if things went wrong, and those issues were unworthy by their very nature because they weren't about him.

Obama's election as the first black president of the Harvard Law Review led to a contract and an advance to write a book about race relations. But guess what, by the end it had evolved into his own autobiography! Instead of writing a scholarly paper focusing on race relations, for which he had been paid, Obama could not resist writing about his most sublime self.

Not surprisingly, Hitler also wrote his own autobiography when he was still a nobody. So did Stalin. For a narcissist no subject is as important as his own self. Why would he waste his precious time and genius writing about insignificant things when he can write about such a majestic being as himself?

Narcissists are often callous and even ruthless. As the norm, they lack conscience. This is evident from Obama's lack of interest in his own brother who lives on only one dollar per month. He has no interest in the plight of his own brother because his brother cannot be used for his ascent to power. A narcissist cares for no one but himself.

The approaching election is like no other in the history of America. What can be more dangerous than having a man void of conscience, a serial liar and one who cannot distinguish his fantasies from reality as the leader of the free world?

I hate to sound alarmist, but you must be a fool if you're not alarmed. Many politicians are narcissists, but they pose no threat to others...they are simply self-serving and selfish. Obama displays symptoms of pathological narcissism, which is different from the run-of-the-mill narcissism of a Richard Nixon or a Bill Clinton for example. To him reality and fantasy are intertwined.

Pathological narcissists are dangerous because they look normal and even intelligent. It is this disguise that makes them treacherous. Today the Democrats have placed all their hopes in Obama. But this man could put an end to their party. The great majority of blacks voted for Obama and will, once again, support him in November 2012.

Obama will set the clock back decades. America is the bastion of freedom. The peace of the world depends on the strength of America, and its weakness translates into the triumph of terrorism and victory for rogue nations. It is no wonder that Ahmadinejad, Hugo Chavez, the Castrists, the Hezbollah, the Hamas, the lawyers of the Guantanamo terrorists, and virtually all sworn enemies of America are thrilled by the prospect of their man in the White House for another four years.

The real downside to all of this is that whether Obama wins or not...America stands to lose. If he's not re-elected the blacks are not likely to give up support for their man. Cult mentality is pernicious and unrelenting. They will dig their heels deeper and accuse Obama detractors of racism. This will cause a backlash among the whites. The white supremacists will take advantage of the discontent and they will receive widespread support. I fear that in less than four years, racial tension could increase to levels never seen since the turbulent 1960s.

If he is re-elected, the possibility of him pushing forward with his desire to disarm and socialize America is conceivable and...would most certainly produce civil unrest.

The ongoing devastation and ignorance being generated and promoted by this presidency could forever destroy the fiber and character of a once great nation. If it is allowed to continue, we will be left with little hope for a course correction or rebuilding...at the present rate of duplicity and complacence being displayed by the American public.

America is on the verge of destruction and there is no greater insanity than re-electing a pathological narcissist as our president.

Government Enabling

In reflecting back on President Franklin Roosevelt's State of the Union address (1941) when he outlined a goal of Four Freedoms: freedom of speech and expression, freedom of people to worship God in their own way, "freedom from want" and "freedom from fear."

He was sowing the seeds of dependence (purposefully or not) over 70 years ago...and today's big government is harvesting the bountiful plunder from that cash crop.

There's a contemporary lie that we don't really need fathers (the growing lack of family structures). The lie is easily exposed for its absurdity because it's no secret that the most violent and impoverished subcultures in the United States are those where fathers are absent. A father's guiding hand and occasional discipline are necessary for children growing up.

Clearly, it's fitting that today we celebrate "Father's Day."

What's not so good is the growing American tendency to seek and even demand a "father figure" long into adulthood. Of course government has gladly...and increasingly embraced that surrogate role as a means of control over the dependent populace.

Many commentators lament the Nanny State, which presumes to nurture us from cradle to grave, as might an overprotective nanny. This is a danger and, unfortunately, also a political trend.

The "Who's your Daddy" phenomenon is even more dangerous. It not only smothers us with parental like dominance, it does so with an iron hand. It's not just a tendency on the left end of the political spectrum, but across all political persuasions. It is the inclination to want a strong, dominating government, not so much to coddle us, but to protect us from life's uncertainties. The irony is, in enfeebling its wards the "State" makes life more precarious, not less so.

FDR infamously proclaimed that we not only have God-given unalienable rights to freedom, as the founders of our nation understood, but that he believed we also should have man-made rights to protect us from nearly everything!

The more of a Nanny State we become, we not only retard our maturation as a society, but become even further enslaved.

The more federal government provides for the people, the more it deprives them not only of their dignity, but of one of the most sacred rights, the right to pursue happiness. Why is that? Because fulfilling happiness comes from earned success, not from unearned handouts.

The more the State does, the less we do for ourselves. You might call it perpetuating adolescence, if not infancy, depending on the degree of submission.

This retarding of cultural maturation is something like spoiling a child...and we've all encountered some of those spoiled children who are arriving at adulthood without a clue or a care. They are the ones acculturated to expect their father, or a surrogate for him, to provide for them. Their reliance outwardly appears to be an attitude of entitlement. But more accurately, it should be known for what it is...utter dependence.

If that weren't bad enough, the Nanny State doesn't just teach people to expect handouts, it also undermines their growth and consequently their ability to fend for themselves.

If ever a politician revealed his core beliefs it was Obama, who professed earlier this year that "this notion that we should have let the auto industry die, that we should pursue anti-worker policies in the hopes that unions like yours will buckle and unravel, that's part of that same old you-are-on-your-own philosophy that says we should just leave everybody to fend for themselves."

Perish the thought that people would fend for themselves, that individuals, companies or institutions should rise or fall based on their own abilities and competences. Not so when the State is in control, Obama tells us.

Most people realize that spoiled children end up unhappy, even if they get everything they want. They know down deep they didn't earn it. They resemble "sucklings" unable to fend for themselves. They end up dependent in a crippling way. Government dominance, even when well intentioned, undermines the individual's pursuit of happiness because it inevitably limits personal responsibility.

It becomes not only someone else's fault if they don't get what they want, but increasingly, it's the government's fault. They also find themselves unable to get it on their own, crippled as they have become in regard to fending for themselves.

The "never-weaned-sucklings" are forever dependent. And the forever dependent dare not rise up and rebel against the State. Not if they want to keep getting their allowances.

EPILOGUE

It occurred to me recently that democracy/freedom is a cyclical phenomenon that mankind has been participating in since the beginning. Democracies and personal freedoms come and go...but there are two commonalities that always accompany these transitions:

> A democracy will "always," over time...succumb to the greed and evil that resides within mankind. As the populace becomes more and more dependent (welfare and other entitlements programs) on their government, the more powerful their government becomes. It is a slow incremental process, but its growth is like an insidious cancer that will spread and consume your life and freedoms...one freedom at a time, until you wake up one morning and realize that your government has morphed into a dictatorship.

> The path back to freedom is "always" facilitated by violence. Around the world...at almost any given time, some country (that was once a free democracy) is struggling to free itself from oppression. America has embraced the role of savior for the whole

world...promoting and sponsoring freedom and democracy for all. The efforts have always been violent, pitting one side again the other...and in most cases, with only superficial changes to show for the destruction and loss of lives. And the cycle just restarts itself...

But in the bigger picture, what are we talking about when we speak of our freedom and/or liberty? Where do we stand when it's broken down to the basics of personal freedom and liberties...for the "individual?" What do we understand about the abstract paradoxical concept of positive liberty and freedom as opposed to negative liberty and freedom?

Isaiah Berlin is popularly known for his essay "Two Concepts of Liberty," delivered in 1958 at Oxford. Berlin argued for a nuanced and subtle understanding of our political terminology, where what was superficially understood as a single concept could mask a plurality of different uses and therefore meanings. Berlin argued that these multiple and differing concepts, otherwise masked by rhetorical conflation, showed the plurality and incompatibility of human values, and the need for us to distinguish and trade off analytically between, rather than conflate them, if we are to avoid disguising underlying value-conflicts. The two concepts are freedom "from" which Berlin derived from the British tradition and freedom "to" which Berlin derived from Rousseau; a Swiss philosopher who *held that the individual is essentially good but usually corrupted by society*. Berlin points out that these two different conceptions of liberty can clash with each other.

Positive liberty, an idea that was first expressed and analyzed as a separate conception of liberty by John Stuart Mill but most notably described by Isaiah

Berlin, refers to the "ability" to act to fulfill one's own potential.

The philosophical concept of negative liberty is the absence of coercion from others. In this negative sense, one is considered free to the extent to which no person or persons interferes with his or her activity. According to Thomas Hobbes, for example, "a free man is he that... is not hindered to do what he hath the will to do."

The idea of positive liberty is often emphasized by those on the "left" of the political spectrum, such as Marxists, whereas negative liberty is most important for those who lean towards the "right"...libertarianism. Positive liberty is often described as freedom to achieve certain ends, while negative liberty is described as freedom from external coercion. Many anarchists, and others considered to be on the "left," see the two concepts of positive and negative liberty as interdependent and thus inseparable.

Berlin himself was deeply suspicious of the concept of positive liberty, noting that totalitarian ideologies such as Stalinist Communism claimed to be the true deliverers of self-mastery or self-realization, even though the individual was by no means free. Berlin argued that the concept of positive liberty could lead to a situation where the state forced upon people a certain way of life, because the state judged that it was the most rational course of action, and therefore, was what a person should desire, whether or not people actually desired it.

"Once I take this view, I am in a position to ignore the actual wishes of men or societies, to bully, oppress, torture in the name, and on behalf, of their 'real' selves, in the secure knowledge that whatever is the true goal of man must be identical with his freedom," Berlin said.

Has Western civilization followed the path of negative

liberty to its logical conclusions for the past 50 years, resulting in a society without meaning, populated by selfish automatons? And have parents, by not wanting to coerce their children into taking a more responsible path...in an effort to allow them to "find" themselves, allowed their immature offspring to embrace the timeless adolescent culture that we're seeing today?

I would suggest that both liberties have their down sides and that it will always come back to the individual...it has, and always will be about personal responsibility, accountability and common sense. Having the "ability" means nothing if one lacks the desire...or is unmotivated because he/she can't be "coerced" or "interfered" with. It's his or her life to do with as they see fit...it's their personal freedom and the government will provide for them if necessary.

In a democracy, the voters determine the reach of their government. Those who value personal freedoms, uphold personal responsibility and recognize the limitations of government actions must speak out against superfluous legislation and support candidates who understand the need for restraint...those who do not view the maximization of legislation as their objective or as a vehicle for political gain.

"We the People" are imperfect. However, it is we as individuals who are the effectual architects and overseers of our circumstances. A society that looks to government as a social watchdog and financial benefactor...rather than to individual responsibility, is not healthy...but in decline. Laws are necessary for an orderly, productive society. Conversely, our preoccupation with government as the prescription for social health has become a destructive obsession.

America is destroying itself from within as its growing

entitlement mentality has morphed into this all consuming human parasite that's willing to sacrifice its host for its short-term, personal gratification. Of course history tells us that our collapse will not represent an anomaly in the rise and fall of great nations since the beginning of time.

The government spends most of its budget writing checks to individuals, not on the military or any other kind of security.

Add up the budget for programs like Social Security, Medicare, food stamps, unemployment benefits, student loans, farmers and veteran's benefits. Direct payments to individuals topped $2.3 trillion dollars, or nearly 66 percent of federal spending last year. Payments to individuals took up only 2.5 percent of the federal budget in 1945.

Behind all of Obama's recent statements lies a bigger issue. He's reinforcing the sense that entitlements are a fundamental right. His latest proposal is a $2.4 billion program to provide cell phones for the poor.

Relief and entitlement programs used to carry a stigma to those who utilized them. But there is no stigma for today's beneficiaries now that it's viewed as a right and not an act of charity.

More than one in five...67 million plus, Americans now rely on government assistance in areas including housing, food, healthcare and schooling. The most recent data indicates government dependency grew by 8.1 percent in 2011. That same data also revealed how the taxpaying population is shrinking, and that half of America's households pay no federal income taxes. As the number of Americans who rely on government subsidies increases, so does the threat to the notion of civil society and close-knit communities.

Dependency isn't necessarily a bad thing, but traditionally those in need have looked to their families, neighbors and churches for help...and those who helped others knew they could count on support if they ever needed help. This dependence is a natural part of life, and builds strength and character in communities.

But...dependence on the government has the opposite effect. With government dependence, a person goes to a bureaucrat and is given aid without any expectation of anything in return. As a consequence, people don't have any incentive to get off welfare, and they're not building personal strength or community bonds. The only thing expanding is the power of the state.

The contemporary psychological reaction is just a shrug... and a head scratch of puzzlement. Food stamp usage surged from 26.3 million in 2007 to 44.7 million at the end of 2011. Today the poor can qualify for food stamps and still enjoy the electronic trappings of a middle class lifestyle that didn't exist two generations ago. As defined in 1965, poverty as we know it in America has been wiped out. Naturally, the government has continued to raise the bar.

The increasing role of entitlements shows a perverse incentive. Rather than acquire a minimum wage job, a basket of benefits can provide the equivalent lifestyle, all while freeing up 40 hours a week. At least under most New Deal programs, there was work to be done.

I'm not saying we should do away with welfare programs. But we've got to restructure them so that the safety net acts more like a trampoline, rather than a retirement home. America will continue losing ground in economic growth and personal freedoms unless we can right our listing ship of fools.

It came to light last week that a Michigan woman, who had won a million dollars in the state's lottery earlier, had continued to collect food stamps. It was only revealed after an investigative reporter followed-up on a tip and his article made the newspaper.

More than anything else, this pretty much sums up the direction our country is heading. If winning such a bonanza didn't motivate the individual to improve herself, what else would? This country became great because of individual accomplishments driven by motivated, prideful individuals.

But the incredible incompetence of our always-expanding governmental system of bureaucracies only exacerbates the problems. I recently read an article about an on-going investigation that "our" unemployment and disability administrators were conducting. They were "looking into the possibility" that some prisoners (yes, more than one... and in prison) had been receiving unemployment and/ or disability checks...for years! It seems the checks were being sent to contacts on the outside who cashed them and then funneled the proceeds back to the recipients in prison.

The Social Security Administration last year reported that the fund would probably run out of money in 2036... or sooner.

The Social Security Administration's separate fund for disabilities will run out of money much sooner, perhaps in 2016, The Wall Street Journal reports.

Can we say, "Ponzi Scheme?"

In December of 1919, Carlo "Charles" Ponzi approached a group of friends and acquaintances, in Boston, with a new investment opportunity. What followed has become immortalized as one of the most infamous investment scams in history.

The similarities between Ponzi's fraudulent investment scheme and our current United States social insurance program are fundamentally the same. The two programs have several commonalities: Social Security does not actually save or invest any of a participant's payments... it relies on the inflow from future contributors to finance the ever-growing system. This provides "a windfall for the first participants, but declining returns for subsequent joiners."

Social Security was a system that worked well when demographics were favorable, but it's currently facing insolvency as the ratio of recipients to contributors continues to escalate.

All the above is comparable to operating a Ponzi scheme.

But despite all their parallels, there is one crucial distinction between the two. "Social Security is not a true Ponzi scheme because Charles Ponzi didn't have a gun." With that said, the debate over epithets obscures a much broader issue: Social Security will be unable to pay promised benefits with current levels of taxation.

As Ronald Reagan used to say, "If you want more of something, subsidize it. If you want less of something, tax it." Today, we subsidize indolence. We tax investment success and wage earners. At the rate entitlements and regulations are increasing, we'll soon be sliding down that rabbit hole into oblivion.

The growth of our government's ineptness is in direct

proportion to its physical growth...parallel tracks, both expanding exponentially. This administration has added hundreds of new departments, regulatory agencies, administrators, czars (autocrats) and is still building... his empire. The logic is, of course, that if enough voters are dependent on the government for their livelihood (government jobs or government entitlements/welfare/subsidies), they will likely give him another four years... the time he needs to complete his mission.

"The American Republic will endure until the day Congress discovers that it can bribe the public with the public's money." Alexis de Tocqueville (1805 - 1859) was a French political thinker and historian best known for his book "Democracy in America." He explored the effects of the rising equality of social conditions on the individual and the state in western societies. It was published in 1835 after his travels in the United States and is still considered an early work of sociology and political science.

> In a time of universal deceit, telling the truth becomes an act of rebellion.

> George Orwell

Epilogue Part II

The Obama administration talks much about sharing the wealth in its mad rush to corral the faltering economy but not much about sharing the labor that creates it. Obama embraces the strategy of "hope," but when hope is your strategy, hope is all you get. The following numbers should point out the frightening demographic trend that *relying on hope leads to...hopelessness.*

There are 311 million people in the United States and according to the United States Department of Commerce, 211 million of them have an income. That doesn't sound so bad until you discover that, according to the United States Department of Labor, only 100.5 million of them are "full time wage and salary workers."

There are, of course, some millions of other part-time or temporary workers but the 100.5 million represent the day-in-day-out, year-in-year-out producers of our economy.

For the first time in United States history, the 100.5 million full-time producers are actually outnumbered by the approximately 111 million people who have an income without a full-time job or even any job.

These good people run the gamut from seniors enjoying a well-earned retirement to unmotivated but well-fed affluent late starters on extended unemployment, the disabled, welfare recipients, part-time workers and a host of others.

That still leaves the 100.5 million full-time workers, right? Not really, because upward of 20 million of them work for the government; that means 80.5 million workers must produce nearly all the goods, services, food, medical care and housing for 311 million, plus pay the 20 million who work in government. They must also provide all the government subsidies, finance the military, pay off the national debt and feed themselves if there's anything left over.

Put bluntly, every private sector, full-time worker supports or subsidizes about 3.8 people. Our government's largely unopposed wealth redistribution policies mean that this number will soon be one in four. By then, there won't be much wealth to share, or as residents of the old Soviet Union used to joke, "The only thing we share is the poverty."

The administration is engaging in "Whack-a-Mole" economics. In the "Whack-a-Mole" arcade game plastic moles randomly pop out of their holes. The player's goal is to whack, with a mallet...as many moles as possible back into their hole. Well, the United States Treasury has decided that it wants to play the game.

In pursuit of his goal for a "level playing field," where the wealthy get punished to offset the plight of the poor, Obama's self-proclaimed wealth-redistribution plan is a high-stakes adaptation of this popular 1976-carnival game.

Unlike the harmless entertainment version, the

Obamanomics adaptation of "Whack-a-Mole" uses the mallet of the tax law to smack wealth-generators whenever they pop their heads up above an arbitrary and capricious income level. So gather around, working-class people, and watch the excitement as your employers, manufacturers, farmers and small businesses get whacked in the name of fairness and equality. Look, an oil company. Whack! Look, a software developer. Whack! Look, a self-employed rich person. Whack! What great fun, whacking capitalists over and over and over.

When we whack moles at the carnival and the game is over, we get to play again. But in Obamanomics, after the whacking is done and the playing field is level, don't be surprised if the carnival packs up the game and leaves town.

PERSPECTIVE

E ven humanity's evolutionary temperament seems to be bending to accommodate the fallout of our distorted view of life today.

I'm going to say right up front that the subject matter I'm about to engage in is contrary to my physical and psychological being. But while the concept is incomprehensible from my vantage point, it's not for me to judge or condemn because I don't walk in their shoes.

There is no disputing the existence of homosexuality (gays and lesbians) in "every culture" since recorded time. Certainly the Romans immediately come to mind, but they were not an anomaly.

The ancient Greeks did not conceive of sexual orientation as a social identifier, as Western societies have done. Greek society did not distinguish sexual desire or behavior by the gender of the participants, but rather by the role that each participant played in the sex act, that of active penetrator or passive penetrated. This active/ passive polarization corresponded with dominant and submissive social roles: The active (penetrative) role was associated with masculinity, higher social status, and adulthood; while the passive role was associated with femininity, lower social status, and youth.

The most common form of same-sex relationships between males in Greece was "paiderastia" meaning "boy love." It was a relationship between an older male and an adolescent youth. A boy was considered a "boy" until he was able to grow a full beard. In Athens the older man was called erastes, he was to educate, protect, love, and provide a role model for his eromenos, whose reward for him lay in his beauty, youth, and promise.

Homosexuality was also common in the Buddhist's monastic life and the Samurai tradition.

Societal attitudes towards same-sex relationships have varied over time and place, from expecting all males to engage in same-sex relationships, to casual integration, through acceptance, to seeing the practice as a minor sin...repressing it through law enforcement and judicial mechanisms, and proscribing it under penalty of death.

Society's acceptance of homosexuality has ebbed and flowed from the beginning, but not it's continuing existence. It has just been forced underground from time to time. But perhaps we're currently seeing a major movement toward legitimizing homosexuality...and I don't just mean in the courtrooms.

A small but growing number of teens and even younger children who think they were born the wrong sex are getting support from parents and from doctors who give them sex-changing treatments, according to reports in the medical journal of Pediatrics.

It's an issue that raises ethical questions, and some experts urge caution in treating children with puberty-blocking drugs and hormones.

An 8-year-old second-grader in Los Angeles is a typical patient. Born a girl, the child announced at 18 months, "I a boy" and has stuck with that belief. The family was shocked, but now refers to the child as a boy and is watching for the first signs of puberty to begin treatment, his mother said.

"Pediatricians need to know these kids exist and deserve treatment, said Dr. Norman Spack. If you open the doors, these are the kids who come. They're out there. They're in your practices."

Switching gender roles and occasionally pretending to be the opposite sex is common in young children. But these kids are different. They feel certain they were born with the wrong bodies.

Some are labeled with "gender identity disorder," a psychiatric diagnosis. But Spack is among doctors who think that's a misnomer. Emerging research suggests they may have brains more similar to the opposite sex.

"Offering sex-changing treatment to kids younger than 18 raises ethical concerns," said Dr. Margaret Moon, a member of the American Academy of Pediatrics' bioethics committee. "Some kids may get a psychiatric diagnosis when they are just hugely uncomfortable with narrowly defined gender roles, or some may be gay and are coerced into treatment by parents more comfortable with a sex change than having a homosexual child. It's harmful to have an irreversible treatment too early," Moon said.

I asked my friend, Gary...who is a pastor, for his opinion on homosexuality with regard to his Christian faith and the Bible.

> He started by saying, "My opinion is not about judgment...nor is it about condemnation."

247

So what is my take on the scriptures that say homosexuality is a sin? I take his desire literally and it concerns me when anyone would attempt to water down the scriptures or take a position that somehow it doesn't mean what it says. Somewhere in all of this, there has to be a place of truth. I have great compassion for the struggle of homosexual men and women; I have equal compassion for anyone who struggles with any sin, sexual or otherwise. However, it does not change the fact that sin, any sin, is not God's desire for us.

Scripture tells us that all the lies of the enemy are built into our lives, line upon line, and precept upon precept. Many people struggle with sin not knowing or remembering how it came to be in their lives.

Behavior is a result of our emotions and our emotions are rooted in what we believe at any given moment. All of us grow up building one conclusion upon another, constructing our beliefs as we go along. These structures are dissimilar from each other and follow relatively unique paths. Take two children raised by alcoholic parents...one builds beliefs that cause them to fear alcohol and never take a drink in their life. The other sees alcohol as an answer to their troubles, an escape from the pain of life. On the surface one may seem healthier than the other, but in reality they are both dysfunctional. Both are rooted in fear...one in fear of alcohol, the other in fear of pain. But both behaviors are learned and developed over a long period of time.

Homosexuality is no different than heterosexual sin or any sin for that matter. It is a path of beliefs built over years of conclusions that are arrived at by misunderstandings of the way to happiness. Of course we don't remember making a decision...we never really did. We believed one thing when we were three years old, then another and pretty soon our emotions were following our beliefs. We never knew what we felt was because of what we believed and so only remember feeling it. Ultimately we gave into that feeling, whether homosexual or heterosexual, it makes no difference. It was the path our beliefs led us down. There is no guilt, no condemnation, only understanding.

The Bible tells me that the Spirit of God will lead me into all truth. It also tells me that the fruit of that truth is love, joy, peace, forbearance, kindness, goodness, faithfulness, gentleness and self-control. If this is true, then it stands to reason, that any emotion contrary to that fruit would be rooted in something other than God's truth. In essence we can say that fear, anger, anxiety, etc. are all the result of lies...something contrary to the truth of God. It is also true that all of those lies and all of those emotions can be generally summed up as fear. The victory is in the fact that perfect love (God's love) casts out (obliterates) all fear. Fear leads us into sin. Somewhere inside we believe that sin offers us something that God cannot. We become afraid that God's way might not be as good for us as our own desires. Because we want happiness and we are afraid that God's way will not make us as happy, we choose sin. We choose unhealthy relationships. We choose drugs, crime, adultery, theft and any number of paths that ultimately lead us to somewhere other than real love.

Paul said, "When I was a child, I spoke and acted as a child, but when I became a man, I put away childish things." This is much more profound than it appears on the surface. It is not just about childish behavior or sin. It is about one's beliefs. Our lives can become a path of discovery and courage to unravel the lies of the past and rebuild based on the truth. It gives us purpose to grow.

In recent years, astonishing technological developments have pushed the frontiers of humanity toward far-reaching morphological transformation that promises in the very near future to redefine what it means to be human. What science has already done with genetically modifying plants and animals will soon apply to Homo sapiens. An international, intellectual, and fast-growing cultural movement known as trans-humanism supports this vision, as does a flourishing list of United States military advisors, bio-ethicists, law professors, and academics. They intend the use of genetics, robotics, artificial intelligence, nano-technology and synthetic biology (Grins technologies) as tools that will radically redesign our minds, our memories, our physiology, our offspring, and even perhaps...as Joel Garreau, in his best selling book "Radical Evolution," claims...our very souls.

Of course, we shouldn't be surprised at our ever-changing world. Hasn't it been in a perpetual state of evolution since the first elements slithered from the water onto the land. It's just that our perspective encompasses such a microscopic sliver of Earth's eternal cycle. But we've always thought of ourselves as the final model... the finished product.

Humankind, being the self-centered species it is, has a tendency to think that the world revolves around them, and that they at their current time period have reached the true apex of civilization, the pinnacle of culture.

An Aesop fable.

I have long pondered intangible thoughts regarding the universe...and I'm not talking about what science tells us. I'm talking about what we don't know, and will never know...in this life. We are limited by what our human minds can fathom...certain concepts are just beyond our comprehension.

Mankind has forever been engaged in the futile effort to ascribe purpose to the universe. But reason just doesn't work. Our minds have evolved to meet the conflicts of survival on a primal level, to eat, to breathe and to avoid monsters (of all types) that would harm us. While intellects have developed the ability to communicate and contemplate things on an abstract level, we still cannot accept concepts such as a beginning without something existing before time and space...and/or the Big Bang theory, nor can we contemplate an ending without anything existing after time and space.

Concepts of eternity and infinity boggle the primitive cognition of our slowly evolving species. What was before the beginning of eternity...and what's after infinity?

It is generally accepted that something cannot come from

nothing. So I pose the question, why is there anything at all...rather than nothing?

Whatever it may be, and however illusory it may seem, something exists. But there is no need for definitive definition, unconditional purpose or complete understanding today...we will know all the answers once our earthly sojourn is concluded.

My friend Gary recently reminded me of what Jesus said before he left:

> "You will hear of wars and rumors of wars, but see to it that you are not alarmed. Such things must happen, but the end is still to come. Nation will rise against nation, and kingdom against kingdom. There will be famines and earthquakes in various places. All these are the beginning of birth pains.
>
> Then you will be handed over to be persecuted and put to death, and you will be hated by all nations because of me. At that time many will turn away from the faith and will betray and hate each other, and many false prophets will appear and deceive many people. Because of the increase of wickedness, the love of most will grow cold, but he who stands firm to the end will be saved. And this gospel of the kingdom will be preached in the whole world as a testimony to all nations, and then the end will come."
>
> Matthew 24 (New International Version 1984)

EPITAPH

America, as my generation knew it...is but an abstract distortion of a time when our country was sustained by the substance of its people. Today's general population seems to live in a vacuum of ignorance and complacency...so for them, substance is often equated to material possessions, rather than character and/or moral fiber. They too often...and mistakenly, look up to celebrities and high profile sports figures as role models. The mainstream media (living in that same vacuum bubble) glorifies and records every aspect of this segment of our populace while keeping Obama propped up on their "see no evil/hear no evil" pedestal.

Irena Sendler, February 15, 1910 – May 12, 2008, was a Polish Catholic social worker that served in the Polish Underground and the Zegota resistance organization in German-occupied Warsaw during World War II. Assisted by some two-dozen other Zegota members, Sendler smuggled 2,500 Jewish children out of the Warsaw Ghetto and then provided them with false identity documents and with housing outside the Ghetto, thereby saving those children from being killed in the Holocaust.

The Nazis eventually discovered her activities, tortured

her, and sentenced her to death; but she managed to evade execution and survive the war. Late in life she was awarded Poland's highest honor for her wartime humanitarian efforts and was also nominated for (but did not win) the 2007 Nobel Peace Prize. She appears on the silver, 2009 Polish commemorative coins honoring some of the Holocaust-resisters of Poland.

And who beat her out for the 2007 Nobel Peace Prize?

Al Gore won for a slide show on Global Warming...and Obama won in 2009 "for his extraordinary efforts to strengthen international diplomacy and cooperation between peoples." In layman's terms Obama earned the award for his "Apologizing for America's Arrogance Tour" with its bowing and ass kissing.

"Don't Cry for Me Argentina," the American version.

The traditional Liberalism held by the likes of Presidents Roosevelt and Kennedy is dead, replaced by a radical left version held by the likes of Barack Obama, Nancy Pelosi and Harry Reid.

In just the last couple of weeks we experienced the following manifestations of this "flexible integrity" Liberalism.

> A United States President, Barack Obama, whose main job is to protect and defend our country, whispered to the out-going Russian president, Dmitry Medvedev, that after he gets re-elected (and free of pretending to care about the American voters) he will give the Russkies a better deal than he dare give them now before "his" election.

> A Liberal Supreme Court Justice, Ruth Ginsberg, whose main job is to protect and defend our Constitution, apparently dislikes it so much that she

advised the Egyptian people not to use the United States Constitution as a model in formulating their new constitution because it was outdated.

➤ And another Liberal Supreme Court Justice, Elena Kagan, who as a member of the Obama team formulated the Obama administration's defense of ObamaCare, didn't recuse herself from participating in the hearing of, and eventually voting on, the constitutionality of the ObamaCare legislation.

It must be said, that like the breaking of a great dam, the American descent into Marxism is happening with breath taking speed, against the backdrop of passive... hapless sheep.

True, the situation has been well prepared for "on and off" over the past century, but especially during the last twenty or thirty years. The initial testing ground was conducted upon Russia and a bloody test it was. But the Russians did not just roll over and give up their freedom and souls, no matter how much money Wall Street poured into the fists of the Marxists.

Those lessons were taken and used to properly prepare the American populace for the surrender of their freedom and souls, to the whims of their elites and betters.

First, the population was dumbed down through a politicized and substandard education system based on pop culture, rather then the classics. Americans know more about their favorite television dramas than the drama in D. C. that directly affects their lives. They care more for their "right" to choke down a McDonalds or Burger King burger than for their "constitutional rights." And they've always excelled at lecturing others on "human rights and democracy." Pride blinds the foolish.

Then their faith in God was destroyed...until their churches, all tens of thousands of different "branches and denominations" became...for the most part, little more then Sunday circuses and their televangelists and top protestant mega preachers were more then happy to sell out their souls and flocks to be on the "winning" side of one pseudo Marxist politician or another. Their flocks complained from time to time, but when explained that they would be on the "winning" side, their flocks were ever so quick to reject Christ in the hope of earthly power. Even the Holy Orthodox churches became scandalously liberalized in America.

The final collapse has come with the election of Barack Obama. His speed in such a short time has been truly impressive. His spending and money printing has been record setting...not just in America's short history, but in the world. If he keeps this pace up for more than another year, and there is no sign that he will not, America... at best, will resemble the Wiemar Republic (Germany's hyperinflation in 1920) or worst case, Zimbabwe today.

These past few weeks have been the most breathtaking of all. First came the announcement of a planned redesign of the American Byzantine tax system, by the very thieves who used it to bankroll their thefts, loses and swindles of hundreds of billions of dollars. They have made the Russian oligarchy look like little more then ordinary street thugs, in comparison. Yes, the current American government has outdone the world-class Russian thieves in the shearing of their populace.

These men are not an elected panel but are appointees picked from the very financial insiders and their henchmen who are now gorging themselves on trillions of American dollars, in one bailout after another. They are also usurping the rights, duties and powers of the

American congress...with congress putting up little more then a whimper to their masters.

Then came Obama's command that the president of General Motors step down from his leadership position with the company. That is correct, dear readers, in the land of "pure free markets," the American president now has the power, the self given power, to fire CEOs and we can assume other employees of private companies, at will. Come hither, go dither, the centurion commands his minions.

So it should be no surprise that the American president has followed this up with a bold move of declaring that he and another group of un-elected, chosen stooges will now redesign the entire automotive industry and will even embody the assurance of automobile policies. I am sure that if given the chance, they would happily try and redesign it for the whole of the world, also. Prime Minister Putin, some months ago, warned Obama and the United Kingdom's Blair, not to follow the path to Marxism because it would only lead them to disaster. Apparently, even though the Russians suffered 70 years of this Western sponsored horror show, their advice means nothing, as foolish, drunken Russians...so let the "wiser" Anglo-Saxon fools find out the folly of their own pride.

Again, the American public has taken this with barely a whimper...but a "free man's" whimper.

So, should it be any surprise to discover that the Democratically controlled Congress of America is working on passing a new regulation that would give the American Treasury department the power to set "fair" maximum salaries, evaluate performance and control how private companies give out pay raises and bonuses? Senator Barney Franks, with his Marxist enlightenment, has led this effort. He stressed that this will only affect companies that receive government monies, but it is retroactive and taken to a logical extreme, this would include any company or industry that has ever received a tax break or incentive.

Foreign owners of American companies and industries should look thoughtfully at this and the option of closing their facilities down and fleeing the land of the Red as fast as possible. In other words, divest while there is still value left.

The proud American will go down into his slavery without a fight, beating his chest and proclaiming to the world, how free he really is. The world will only snicker.

I can't help but be reminded of Abraham Lincoln's foreboding prophecy: "America will never be destroyed from the outside. If we falter and lose our freedoms, it will be because we destroyed ourselves."

James Madison, the primary author of the Constitution of the United States, said this: "We have staked the whole future of our new nation, not upon the power of government; far from it. We have staked the future of all our political constitutions upon the capacity of each of ourselves to govern ourselves according to the moral principles of the Ten Commandments."

Today we are asking God to bless America. But how can He bless a Nation that has departed so far from Him?

Just a bird's eye view of the quagmire below...

About the Author:
Richard McKenzie Neal

*One should never equate education
and/or intelligence to wisdom...*

Richard was born in Hope, Arkansas (Bill Clinton's boyhood home), in 1941 and his father was gone prior to Richard turning two years old. He never knew the man, but attended his funeral as a sixteen-year-old.

Before boarding a Greyhound bus for California, at seventeen, Richard knew two stepfathers and a number of others who were just passing through. During those teen years, before succumbing to the beckoning allure of the outside world, Richard worked at an assortment of low-paying jobs. Summers were spent in the fields... picking cotton and/or watermelons and baling hay. He also worked as a plumber's helper and a carhop at the local drive-in burger stand.

After dropping out of school, eloping and landing in California, he soon realized how far out of his element he had ventured. And without the guidance of his "Constant Companion," Richard would have spent a lifetime floundering in a sea of ignorance and ineptness...and his books would not exist.

Richard's first book (Fridays With Landon) was driven by his son's life-altering heroin addiction. He had hoped not to author a sequel, but left the book open-ended due to historical concerns, which did in fact...resurface. For 25 years the family has endured the emotional highs and lows associated with the chaotic, frustrating and more often than not...heartbreaking task of rescuing one of their own, from the always ebbing and flowing tide of addiction.

The unintended sequel (The Path to Addiction...) was triggered by a mind-numbing relapse after 30 months of sobriety. The second book was then written to bring closure...one-way or the other. The author advanced several possible scenarios for the ending of that book, but only one of those possibilities was favorable.

His third book (The Long Road Home...) is a philosophical journey that we'll all experience as our time here begins to dwindle.

The fourth book (We the People) was driven by what he saw as the dismantling of America and the circumventing of its Constitution. Additionally, the ominous cloud of socialism and a New World Order looming over Washington motivated him to speak up, in spite of political correctness' muzzle.

The fifth book (The Compromising of America) was written to confirm and document the realities of those fears and concerns chronicled in the preceding book. While those fears and concerns were driven by the current administration, his nightmare now is the possibility of that same administration being returned to office, for another four years, in 2012. He has grave apprehension regarding America's future should the unthinkable happen.

This book completes the trilogy...and will speak for itself.

All six books were written after retiring from a rewarding, thirty-six years in the oil industry.

Our success should be measured by what we gave up (what it cost us) to obtain it...and not by what we accomplished and/or accumulated.

Richard McKenzie Neal

Vancouver Island

Contributors:

Victoria Davis

Gary

Venita Myers

Judith Neal

Shirley (Morton) Smith

Debra Stone